Seeing
for
Ourselves

Seeing *for* Ourselves

Biblical Women Who Met Jesus

Katerina Katsarka Whitley

MOREHOUSE PUBLISHING

Morehouse Publishing
P.O. Box 1321
Harrisburg, PA 17105

Morehouse Publishing is a division of The Morehouse Group.

Cover design by Wesley Hoke

Cover art: Frederiksborg Castle Church, Denmark. *The Woman of Samaria* by Heinrich Bloch (1834–1890).

Library of Congress Cataloging-in-Publication Data

Whitley, Katerina Katsarka.
    Seeing for ourselves : the women who met Jesus / Katerina Katsarka Whitley.
        p.   cm.
    ISBN 0-8192-1890-1
    1. Women in the Bible—Meditations. 2. Bible. N. T.—Meditations.
    I. Title.

BS2445 .W48 2002
225.9'22'082—dc21

                                                            2001042597

Printed in the United States of America

01 02 03 04 05 06   6 5 4 3 2 1

To my mother Persephone, who died at 36

"Where, Oh death, is your victory?
Where, O death, is your sting?"

Contents

Acknowledgments ix
Introduction 1

1. A Wedding Gift Like No Other 7
The Bride of Cana Remembers Her Wedding Day

2. Water for the Parched Soul 15
The First Evangelist Tells Her Story

3. Dancing with the Lord of Life 21
The Daughter of Jairus Remembers
   Her Visit to the Other Side

4. I Am the One Who Touched His Cloak 29
A Story Told to Gentiles

5. An Alabaster Jarful for My Life 37
A Forgiven Woman Offers Her Gratitude
   and Remembers the One Who Changed Her Life

6. Finding My Heart's Desire 45
Mary of Bethany Tells of Her Encounter With Jesus

7. Remembering the Human Jesus 53
Martha Describes the Days in Bethany

8. There Was No Death in the Man Jesus 63
Pilate's Wife Speaks before a Christian Assembly in Rome

9. In the Breaking of the Bread   71
Cleopas's Wife Celebrates the Remembrance of
    Holy Community with New Christians

10. The Visit of the Comforter   79
Prisca Recounts to Paul Her Own Encounter with Christ

11. Walking in the Light as a Servant of Christ   89
Phoebe Introduces Herself to a New Family of Believers

12. Seeing the Face of Christ in Those of the Redeemed 99
A Young Woman Encourages Believers in Thessaloniki
    During the Time of Nero's Persecution of Christians

Bibliography   109

Acknowledgments

To every church and every group that issued me an invitation to share the stories of *Speaking for Ourselves,* I offer thanks. To the women of Christ Church, Raleigh, North Carolina, who invited me to their vibrant parish to share the resurrection stories of my novel-in-progress, I give thanks. Your reaction to them persuaded me to write this book.

To my editor Debra Farrington, who once again saw the value of these stories and welcomed them with enthusiasm as she did those of the first book, I owe much gratitude. And to Val Gittings, who came up with the thoughtful discussion questions at the end of every chapter—thanks for going to the heart of the stories.

To my dear husband who always believes in me, provides me with the leisure to write, and accompanies me to the many churches I visit, my undying love. And to my Greek family whose faith has always inspired me—I do not ever forget you.

To all women of faith who challenge and inspire me, those who are now on the other side and those who remain here, I sing a song of praise to God for all of you.

Introduction

When I wrote, *Speaking for Ourselves: Voices of Biblical Women*, I thought I had dealt with all the women in the Bible who had fascinated me since my youth. After the publication of the book, I was invited to speak on those twelve women, and I became so accustomed to their voices that I could put on their personas at will. Because of the distinct seasons of the church calendar, Mary, the mother of Jesus, Elizabeth, the mother of John the Baptizer, Mary Magdalene, the witness to the resurrection, came to be the favorites of congregations assembled for Advent, Epiphany, Lent, and Easter. I always feel that I am entering holy ground when I speak during these seasons of the year; I thank all those who offered me the pulpit.

What gave me special satisfaction as a dramatist and as a woman was the connection with groups of women who were willing to talk about the lesser-known personalities in that book: Tamar, the daughter of David; Gomer, Hosea's wife; even Miriam the prophet who, though famous, is rarely acknowledged. During those intimate times, I would hear words that astonished and disturbed me. A young woman in a Catholic parish group saying about the raped Tamar: "I have been there. I understand her." An older woman speaking about the relationship of Tamar with her father: "I could not have forgiven King David. It was very difficult to forgive my mother, and it happened only as she was dying." How contemporary these ancient stories became at such moments, and how healing the discussions that followed. It has been deeply satisfying to see women of our day struggle with their problems by the light of those who left us examples of faith and endurance in the Scripture stories. I remember a young mother telling me: "With two little ones at home and a brand new baby, it was so comforting to read about the Virgin Mary and to see her as a mother like me!"

I thank God for every woman I encountered in the Bible and for every woman who came up to me and said, "I will never read these stories in the same old way ever again. You gave me a new way to look at them. These women are alive for me now." The ultimate satisfaction has been to hear people say that the persons in Scripture came alive for them because of the incarnational way in which I approached their stories.

Meanwhile, I continued reading and listening. Through books and conversations, I realized that many Christians have lost the assurance of the resurrection. I noticed a casual, dismissive attitude about the person of Jesus Christ. It may be the fault of contemporary biblical scholarship such as the Jesus Seminar or simply human hubris—the conviction of many writers that they are so much smarter than the writers of the Scriptures that nothing in the biblical text holds true for them any longer.

Many of the critics are writers I admire. I kept asking myself: Do we read the gospel stories as if Homer or Plato wrote them? Or do we allow the Holy Spirit to reveal the truth of the resurrection with the awe, amazement, and conviction that came to the first women on Easter morning at the empty tomb? I have concluded that we cannot be convinced of the resurrection on human terms only; we need the intervention of the Holy Spirit. So I started looking at the women who met Jesus face-to-face—and the ones who came to know him through other Christians in that dangerous first century of the new faith—to see how they were changed: What happened to them after an encounter with Jesus or with the glorified Christ of Saint Paul? The more I read and wrote, the more I came to be convinced anew that a person like the human Jesus could not have been invented or imagined by the people of the time. The gospel stories have the authenticity of eyewitnesses. There are details in almost all of them that could not have been invented. Those of us who write stories recognize their truth immediately.

Initially, I had simply wanted to look at the women who were confronted by the empty tomb. When I shared their stories with groups of assembled Christians, however, I was overwhelmed by my listeners' desire to hear more, to hear stories of the radical transformation of those who met Jesus both before his death and after his resurrection.

In response to these desires, I started looking specifically at women who met Jesus, women whose lives were altered from that moment on. I came away with the longing to know more about who they were *before* and what happened to them *after* that life-changing encounter. For I am persuaded that no one is confronted by Jesus without a radical alteration of life and thought. I read the story of the first evangelist, the Samaritan woman, over and over—and I started knowing her. Then I decided to look at others who are unnamed; for example, why did a woman come to a banquet given by a Pharisee to wash Jesus' feet with her tears or to anoint him with nard? What brought on such enormous gratitude? What about the little girl Jesus brought back from death, Jairus's daughter? She is not named but her story is so vivid. With her mother and father in the room and with Jesus' most trusted friends near him, he utters the words, so human, so unexpected, "Give her something to eat." Whom did the little girl recognize during and after her experience on the other side?

Therefore, the stories in this book unfolded as resurrection stories, stories of the first witnesses who make it possible for us, two thousand years later, to believe. But what about those who came later, who truly knew Jesus only through the Holy Spirit? What difference did the Pentecost make? Since Paul hardly ever refers to the human Jesus, what was the vision of the resurrected Lord that grasped his life and never let it go? What of the women who came to Jesus through Paul or who helped him in his great missionary endeavors, including Prisca, Phoebe, and many of the others mentioned by him only by name, with great love and gratitude? I had to find out how they came to be pillars of strength for Paul. Their resurrection stories resemble our own encounter with the living Lord—through the witness of the Holy Spirit. Only through the Holy Spirit are we able to pray; it is through the Holy Spirit that we are convinced of the resurrection.

A Word About Dramatic Monologues

As with my first book, the dramatic monologue appeals to me in the telling of these stories. I have longed to hear the voices of the women recounting what happened to them when they encountered Jesus *in the manner of women*. The details women choose to remember are usually different from those that men remember. In every encounter, women's feelings are paramount while the mind remains active. The heart is always touched in some way. Gratitude is so much a part of a woman's life. Noticing someone's face, the pain or sadness in the eyes, the tired look of someone who helps us, the quality of the voice—all these are details women pay attention to. I wanted to hear their voices, their feelings, and the details they focused on—the dramatic monologue is the best genre for this kind of retelling.

In a dramatic monologue, there is always only one voice speaking to an implied audience whom we do not see but to whom the narrator responds. The freedom I have taken in retelling these biblical stories is simply that of a dramatist and, I pray, of a redeemed imagination.

A Note on the Use of Names

As a Greek who grew up with the familiar names of the New Testament in the original language, I prefer the Greek pronunciation in most instances. I avoid using an alternative unless a name is so ingrained in the consciousness of my readers that the Greek would be confusing. Additionally, I prefer the Greek ending –os- to the Latin –us- in names that have a Greek origin; for example, Olympos instead of Olympus.

People who have grown up in liturgical churches are familiar with the expression *Kyrie eleison,* the Greek for "Lord, have mercy." However, they may not be able to make the connection with the nominative of the form, "O Kyrios!" (The Lord!) which is found in the monologue, "In the Breaking of the Bread." To my ears it is much more powerful than "The Lord"; therefore, I used it on that occasion.

Timotheos means "he who honors God," one word that says it all; I used it instead of Timothy in the monologue set in my hometown, Thessaloniki.

ONE

A Wedding Gift Like No Other

THE BRIDE OF CANA REMEMBERS HER WEDDING DAY

John 2:1–11

The evangelist John is the only one who tells this story. It comes immediately after the calling of Jesus' disciples and its significance lies in its being the first miracle recorded by John whose time sequence Archbishop Temple considers the most reliable among the gospels. Its importance seems to be in the impression this miracle made upon those who had already decided to follow Jesus. Years later, when rumors of this miracle prompt new Christians to ask her about it, the bride focuses on Jesus' impression on her. I owe a debt of gratitude to Dorothy L. Sayers for her book The Man Born to Be King *and Archbishop Temple for helping me visualize the scene in his book* Readings in Saint John's Gospel. [Dr. William Temple (1881–1944) was Archbishop of York (1929–1942) when he wrote *Readings in St. John's Gospel* (1939). He served as Archbishop of Canterbury from 1942 until his death two years later.]

I didn't know when I woke up that morning that my wedding would become the talk of Galilee in years to come. I was from Nazareth and my husband-to-be from Cana. It was the day of his arrival. He was coming with the wedding party to take me to his home. His family was rather well-off and I was very apprehensive about meeting his mother and living in her home from that day forward. I knew that the first part of my life had ended and that the second was about to begin. I woke up early, sat up in bed, and tried to take in great gulps of air. I found I couldn't breathe. Something like panic seized me. My mother and sisters came in to dress me and found me gasping for breath. They started laughing—instead of having compassion for me—and then I began to cry and laugh and the panic passed. *(She laughs at the memory.)*

"Every bride feels this way, silly," my older sister said, and that calmed me down. I didn't want them to think I was afraid to get married. Nothing was worse than being unwanted; I had been told this all my young life. But I loved being home in Nazareth. I didn't want to leave everyone and everything I knew for a man I had hardly ever seen, except in furtive looks from behind a screen when he could not see me. What if he didn't like what he saw when he lifted my veil? What if his mother was difficult to live with? I was very worried but ashamed to express my fears.

The women had bathed me and had laid out my wedding clothes when a friend of my mother's came in to see how we were getting along. I had known her only as Mariam, the wife of Joseph the carpenter, but she had a large family, like ours, and kept close to home most of the time. She was my mother's friend, so I was pleased when she came to wish me well. We had heard that her oldest son, Yeshua, Jesus, had left home and the carpentry shop of his father a month before to become a rabbi. There were rumors that he was a prophet. He and my oldest brother had played together as children, so it seemed very strange to all of us to think that we had known a playmate who was a prophet.

I heard my mother say, "Mariam, dear, you must miss him very much," and I guessed they were talking about Jesus. Mariam's voice rose in a happy laughter. "Oh, my dear, but I am especially happy today. Jesus is coming to the wedding. He has been invited by the bridegroom. It seems that they met each other recently and your new son invited *my* son to the wedding feast. Isn't this a happy day for all of us? I am going on ahead to help with the preparations." And then their voices faded as my mother bade her goodbye.

I looked down at my dress and felt a shiver go through me. A prophet coming to my wedding feast? How amazing. Still, using the word prophet for someone we knew sounded impossible, and I put it out of my mind.

When dear Jonah arrived with his large party, I was ready. Everyone was running around to make sure we had all the dowry properly assembled and loaded on the donkey, the girls were squealing at the sight of so many young men, and then Jonah found me alone for a moment. He came near me and, making sure no one was looking, he lifted a corner of the veil, looked me straight in the eye, and smiled at me. I knew then that all would be all right. He had such a lovely, warm smile. He squeezed my hand, and then we got ready and joined the procession. *(She smiles fondly at the recollection.)*

All of that seems like a dream now. The long walk from Nazareth to Cana, the laughter and the jokes of the bridesmaids, the teasing of the young men, the sudden songs, the sun warm on my head and back, my mother touching me and wiping her eyes every now and then. I kept looking for Jonah as he moved among the young people of the procession, making sure all was well, and I kept hoping that the one brief moment of communion between us foretold good things for us in our life together.

When Cana came into sight it was nearly evening, and servants ran with torches from Jonah's lovely courtyard to lead us to the house that would become my home. We were welcomed with great warmth and I felt like the guest of honor for just a few minutes, seated near my new mother- and father-in-law with Jonah close to me. But that didn't last long. Suddenly there was a great commotion in the court- yard and I heard Mariam, my mother's friend, exclaim: "It's Jesus. He has finally arrived." And everyone turned away from me and Jonah to gaze at the young prophet.

He looked the same as ever—a very strong, arresting face with amazing eyes, very simple in his robes, with those pow- erful carpenter's arms of his free and bare, his strides long as he walked on the tiled, cool floor. But he was not alone. He was followed by a group of men who seemed to be enthralled by him, a group that obviously upset his mother.

The commotion quieted as the head servant called out orders to the rest of the help for more couches and tables and finally everyone was seated. Good wishes and speeches started while cups were filled again and again with wine. I looked through my diaphanous veil and remained quiet. My nervousness had almost left me because the whole scene was so fascinating. All those men talking at the same time and then suddenly stopping when the son of Mariam opened his mouth. There was nothing of the scary prophet of doom about him. He laughed with his friends and seemed to enjoy the herbs and wine and the aromatic bread. As the meat on the spit was served, the laughter got louder and I heard Jonah's father asking the steward for more wine. The steward ran toward the wine jars and the servants attending them and I saw him pull back as they shook their heads. He looked very angry. Mariam happened to be passing by the servants at that time—she was bringing a tray from the kitchen and heading toward the table where Jesus and his friends sat—and she stopped to talk to one of the servants. I saw her look alarmed, and then with renewed purpose she approached her son. "Do something," I heard her say, "They have run out of wine." He lifted his eyes and looked at her and all conversation stopped around them. As the whispering died down I heard some of his words clearly: "My time has not yet come." Again, I felt a shiver go through me, and Jonah turned to me and asked in a soft voice, "Are you not well, my love?" I smiled under my veil and reached and touched his hand secretly to reassure him. "Something very strange is happening at that table," I whispered.

We both looked and saw Mariam approach the servants, say something to them, and point toward her son. A few moments passed. Then Jesus stood and walked toward the entranceway looking all around him. He stopped in front of the six large stone jars that stood by the door empty, ready for the household's purification rites. He looked at them without moving while, urged by his mother, several of the servants went over and stood close to him. I saw him point to the jars as the words "Fill the jars with water" formed on his lips. The servants again seemed confused, but they ran away, came back with clay water pots, and poured their contents into the stone jars. It took a few minutes to fill them all. Jonah and I stopped eating and watched. No one else seemed much concerned with what was going on, but I saw Jesus' friends looking at him, riveted by his every move. I noticed the youngest one of them, whose name, I later learned, was John, looking as if he was thunderstruck. And I thought: He is shivering, as I am. Something is going on here that is beyond all we have known before. *(Her voice recalls the awe of the moment.)* There was a trembling in the air as before a thunderstorm. I felt as though the earth was shaking under my feet; I feared an earthquake, but no one except John seemed to be feeling it. I could see it on his face and in the way he held onto his older brother.

The steward appeared again, calling the servants. I saw
Jesus telling them to draw from the jars. One of them
plunged the dipper and brought out not water but a golden
liquid that glowed in the lamplight as he poured it in a carrying jar. The servant brought it to the steward, who poured
it in a cup and, lifting it to his lips, tasted it. I saw him pause
in surprise and smack his lips, in the manner of wine stew-
ards, but he looked puzzled. He approached my Jonah. "Sir,"
he said, "I apologize that it took so long. There seems to be
some confusion. At every feast I have ever served the master
brings the good wine out first; then, after the guests are
drunk, he brings out the inferior wine. But you, sir, you kept
the very best for the last. And it *is* the best. Most unusual."

Jonah tasted the wine and turned to me. I saw that his
face was full of questions. When the steward left, I whispered: "Have you heard that your guest Jesus is a prophet?"

"Yes," he said. "I was so drawn to him when I heard him
speak in Capernaum that I went right up to him and invited
him to our wedding feast. Did you notice what happened?"
I nodded. I could not speak. Who would ever believe me if I
told them this story?

I looked at every guest very carefully. I wanted to take the
moment and imprint it in my mind and in my heart for ever
and ever. I have forgotten so much of my long life, but not
that moment. Everything is as clear as the night I witnessed
it. I saw the members of my new family smiling and looking
at me with welcome in their eyes. I felt Jonah's eyes on me
and I longed for the time we would be alone together and
would learn to know and love one another. I saw the servants
looking after the guests and stopping every now and then to
whisper among themselves and to point to Jesus with something like fear on their faces. I saw Mariam, his mother, with

tears in her eyes. Had she remembered something? Had she recognized something? She did not seem the same woman I had seen that very morning.

Most of all I looked at Jesus and at his friends. He had returned to their table and had picked up a morsel of food to put in his mouth. But it remained in his hands. John was talking to him earnestly and the other men leaned closer to listen, their eyes full of love and admiration for their friend and rabbi. I saw Jesus lift up his eyes toward heaven, something I would see him do again and again in the months to come, then reach out his hands to place them briefly on each of his followers. One he touched on the hair, the other on the hand, another on the shoulder, as though to reassure them, to comfort them. Something extraordinary had happened and he was telling them that it was good, that they were not to be afraid. I held all these images in my heart. No one had ever received a better wedding present.

As the celebration and the feasting continued, the time arrived for Jonah to lead me to the interior of the house. Jesus approached our table. Jonah immediately stood up and said, "Master, I thank you for honoring our wedding day with your presence." Jesus looked at him and smiled; he placed his hand on Jonah's shoulder, as comrades do. Then he looked at me. I knew his eyes could see me clearly through my veil. I did not lower my head. I could not keep from looking into those eyes so full of love and strength, something I could not escape. "When the time comes," he said, "follow me."

Much later, when I asked Jonah if he heard those words, Jonah was surprised. "No," he said. "He didn't say anything to you. How could you think that?" *(She shakes her head in wonder.)* But I had heard Jesus' words clearly. And I gave him a promise that he alone heard. I have kept my promise.

Questions to Ponder
1. Recall times of great transition in your life. Did you feel free to express your fears during those times? Why or why not?
2. Identify the various fears of the characters in this story. In what ways does Jesus respond to them?
3. Have you ever felt comforted or calmed by the presence of Jesus? How do you think such feelings came about?
4. Why did Jesus choose this miracle to be his first after he said, "My time has not yet come?"
5. Why are John and the bride the only ones aware of what is happening?

TWO

Water for the Parched Soul

THE FIRST EVANGELIST TELLS HER STORY

John 4:7–42

This story is full of details. It is Jesus' only proclamation that he is the Messiah. It is found only in John's Gospel and is remarkable because it is made to a woman who is an outcast, a Samaritan.

I didn't like my neighbors. They watched me, and they snickered. All my life I had felt their eyes upon me—from the women, looks of hatred and envy; from the men, looks of longing and greed. They all wanted something from me, and it wasn't the brilliance of my mind. So I came to despise them all—the men for their rapaciousness; the women for their jealousy that never let them guide me or teach me what to do with the beauty that was thrust on me at birth. I had not chosen to look the way I did, so I took revenge on all of them. Women lost sons and husbands to me; men lost me.

On that day—I cannot talk about it without crying inside—I took my jug and bucket and slithered downhill to Jacob's well. It was high noon, when the earth and those not in shade felt parched. I was the only one who went to the well in the heat of the day. I did not want to meet my neighbors in the cool of the morning and evening, although I was always thirsty during those days. Thirsty, but never cooled

15

enough to stop longing for water, no matter how much I drank. Everything I knew about myself was physical; it had to do with my body. You have to keep that in mind to understand what happened to me that day.

From a distance I saw him sitting by the well. He was so still that I couldn't make out whether he was asleep or awake. But I could tell that he was a Jew, not one of our own. He wasn't looking at me. I think his eyes were open, but he seemed in another world. I was determined that he would notice me. I wasn't used to being ignored by men. So I walked directly in front of him, making a big to-do about lowering the jug from my head and sighing a deep sigh.

He still did not look at me, but I heard his voice say, "Give me a drink of water." He sounded travel weary. There was nothing in his manner to remind me of other men. He kept his eyes averted, in the respectful way of men speaking to respectable women. It took me by surprise. I was half pleased and half angry at being ignored. I went on the attack. "You are a Jew. How is it that you ask *me* for a drink? I am a Samaritan woman."

He looked at me then. There was a little smile in the corners of his eyes, but sadness on his face. The eyes said to me, "It is all right that you are a woman. You don't have to apologize for it." But his voice said, "Oh, if you only knew the gift of God! If you only knew who it is who is asking you for a drink of water! You would have asked me, and I would have given you *living* water."

I took my empty bucket, tied the rope on its handle, and dropped it into the well. I felt again the gnawing in my stomach, the dryness in my mouth. How did he know of my constant thirst? I heard the words "living water" and in an instant remembered the thousand of times I had walked to this well, the unending weight on my head and shoulders from carrying the heavy, filled jugs. I wanted that living water, but I couldn't give in to a Jew. I started arguing with him. "I brought the bucket with me," I said. "You had no way of getting water from the deep well. Are you greater than our ancestor Jacob?" I thought, while I was at it, I might as well give him some history lessons. "Do you know that our ancestor Jacob gave us this well and he and his flocks drank from it?" I saw him laughing to himself as if I had told him something about a relative of his that amused him.

Then he looked into my eyes, and all my silliness disappeared. No one else seemed to matter to him at that moment. He put his hand on the rim of the well. "Everyone who drinks of this water will be thirsty again," he said, and I felt the terrible dryness in my throat. "But those who drink from the water that I give them will never be thirsty again. It will become a spring of water gushing up to eternal life."

I wanted to fall on my knees. I wanted to cry out, "Please, give me this water that doesn't end!" But I controlled myself and said it very calmly. "Please give it to me. Then I can stop coming back and forth to draw this water." I kept lying to myself and I knew it. Something else was going on here, but I was going to ignore it as long as I could.

He said, very quietly, "Go, call your husband, and come back here."

Then I told him the truth: "I have no husband," and the emptiness of my life yawned before me. A woman in our part of the world has no respect without a husband. And I had not been given any children. He continued to look at me, without contempt, as he told me the story of my life. I was stunned. "Are you a prophet?" I asked. Before he could answer, I felt myself being gripped by something I had never felt before. This would be for life, I thought, and it has nothing to do with my body. This will be for life. Frightened of what was to come, I decided to argue with him. I challenged him about places of worship and about other long-standing arguments between Jews and Samaritans. But he would not be swayed. None of that mattered to him. He was determined to give me the living water of his words. He was determined to offer me the reality of the spirit, not of the body. He compelled me to think of truth, not of evasions. With the power of his personality, he forced me to see beyond the well and the mountain, beyond my resentments and flirtations, beyond the evil done to me to the evil I had done to others. I said in desperation, "I know that the Messiah is coming, the one called the Christ; when he comes, he will announce everything to us." He answered unequivocally: "I am he, the one talking to you."

I dropped the bucket, I left the jar, and I ran to the village. For the first time I was willing to meet with my neighbors. I was going to face their disdain and their hypocrisies, and I was not going to cringe. I had news! I stood in the middle of the square and said, in a voice that carried, "I have met a prophet by the well of Jacob." I heard them laughing. But I too could be persuasive. I added, "He told me everything that I have ever done." Then they emerged from the shadows. They surrounded me. They were skeptical, but they were also interested. All of us longed for the Messiah. I told them this could be the one. Did they care to find out? We all ran to the well. We all longed for living water.

He came and stayed with us for a few days despite the objections of his friends. He came because of me; but he stayed for everybody's sake.

I still have to go to the well to get water for my family. But now I am never thirsty. I drink on his words. I drink of his spirit. I remember everything he told me and I am filled. I have even come to love my neighbors. The women walk to the well with me. Our husbands and children wait for us to give them not only the cool water of the well, but also the living water of what we learned from him. Although I no longer see him, I know he is with me always. I am no longer a prisoner of my body but a woman free. I drink now of the gushing spring of the eternal.

Questions to Ponder

1. Why do you think Jesus chose a woman (and a Samaritan besides) as the first person to whom he revealed himself as the Messiah?

2. Put yourself in this woman's place. Would you have felt the same way she did toward her neighbors before she met Jesus? Why or why not? How would you have reacted to a man telling you about all the things you have ever done?

3. Would your feelings toward your neighbors have changed after your encounter with Jesus? Why or why not?

4. Have you encountered Jesus as the Christ of God? The Greeks call repentance *metanoia*, change of mind. Has your mind changed about Jesus? How has that affected your feelings toward others?

THREE

Dancing with the Lord of Life

THE DAUGHTER OF JAIRUS REMEMBERS HER VISIT TO THE OTHER SIDE

Matthew 9:18–26
Mark 5:21–43
Luke 8:41–56

This story, with minor variations, is told by Matthew, Mark, and Luke. In each instance, it includes the story of the woman suffering from a hemorrhage. It gives us some clues about Jesus' feelings toward familial bonds of love.

What do I remember about him? That he is the Lord of Life. Isn't that enough? I look at your eyes and see that you don't know what I mean when I say "the Lord of Life." Is it possible for those of you who never saw him on this earth to open your eyes enough to see him now? *(She peers at her audience as though examining them.)*

What happened to me—and I'm told there are only a handful of people who would know my meaning—what happened when he visited my childhood home didn't give me any special privileges, you see, just life, life. Ach, how does one go back to that moment? You may think I never forget it, but I do. Most of the time, I don't think about it. Then something happens, like the illness of my granddaughter, and I am

21

back again in that room choking with lack of air, under a blanket of fever, tossing on my narrow bed.

We were a privileged family, we of the household of Jairus, my dear father. Abba was a big man in the synagogue, and with that came the good things of life. Our home in Galilee was comfortable and large, and we observed with gratitude the law of the Lord God of Israel. What I loved best about my father was that he never told me he was sorry not to have a son. I was his only child, a daughter, and he loved me. That was not true of all my friends. Some of them would come to play with me just to see how it felt to be a girl and to be loved.

I had a happy childhood and was cherished by my parents. I never thought I would leave Galilee. Capernaum, my home, was lovely, there by the sea, and I was like a little fish, jumping in and out of the water whenever I could escape the vigilance of my nurse and mother. My knees and bottom were always red from scraping them on the rocks. I remember waking up in the early morning and looking at the glistening surface of the lake and thinking how good it was to be Jairus's daughter and to live in Capernaum. The smells of the sea and of the wildflowers that grew all over the shore are still with me. That love for all things beautiful is what gave me the illness that almost killed me . . . well, it did kill me. Isn't that what you came to hear? *(She laughs, and then begins to paint a picture of a moment that is imprinted in her memory.)*

It was one of my days of escape. Two of my friends had come to see me and we gave the slip to the nurse, climbed down the rocks, and headed for the sea. A light on the water fascinated me—I had seen it from my window at night, so I needed to investigate. We walked for a long while. We had to reach the part of the shore that was empty of fishermen, because it was not proper for us girls to be seen. We ended up quite far from our house, hidden from curious eyes. I dived in the water and immediately something hit me with such a fierce sting that I knew I was dying, right then and there. I don't know how I managed to scream, but my friends must have heard the sound and they knew that I was not fooling. They both jumped in. Between them, they dragged me to the shore. The sun was beating down on us, but I was shaking all over. Every bit of my body was howling with pain. My friends didn't know what to do. I couldn't speak, but somehow, before I lost consciousness, I made them understand that they had to go for help. One of them ran to the house, while the other stayed with me. She was terribly frightened. By then I was in too much pain to care what the nurse and mother would say. Soon I didn't know what was happening around me. I learned later that all the servants, summoned by my friend, ran to me as fast as they could and carried me to the house. *(Now she recalls things she experienced as an observer only.)*

I remember my mother's touch on my fevered face and how good that felt. I kept begging for water to drink. I was so hot and cold at the same time. My head was throbbing, I couldn't get enough air, my legs no longer worked, and I kept mumbling and tossing on my bed. Whenever I opened my eyes, there was my mother looking out of her mind with worry. I knew she was scared for me because she hadn't said a word about my escapade on the lake. My mouth was so dry that I thought my tongue had become a stick of wood. Someone must have gone to fetch my father, for I suddenly heard his voice asking urgent questions of my mother. The local physician was there too, but he kept shaking his head.

I heard the words "poison in her blood . . . a demon in the water," but nothing he did was helping me.

I was drifting into a place where I did not want to go. I wanted them to keep on talking because I could hear them, although I couldn't speak. I thought their voices were holding me here, holding me back from a place I did not want to enter. Suddenly I heard my father's voice say, "The prophet Jesus is back in Capernaum. I shall go to him for help." And he left the room.

Time passed. The fever was burning me. I couldn't breathe. I heard my mother's weeping, and then nothing. What I remember next is very difficult to describe, and you need to forgive me for that. We don't have the words, you see. *(Now she is in a place we cannot enter. Her eyes and ears are filled with something we cannot imagine, and she knows it. Her voice is dreamy.)*

There was a sunny field full of flowers and laughter and a kind of dancing. I have tried for years to describe that dancing, but it cannot be done. There are no words . . . because even the words were dancing, and the songs were dancing, and the feelings were dancing. *(She is caught in a memory that is like a trance.)*

The voices were those of happy children, and I felt so much at home among them, so happy, so happy! The fever was gone. I didn't even remember the terrible burning pain that had attacked me. I kept looking around me, searching for someone, I think. There seemed to be a center to all this joy, and the dancing seemed to be happening around this center. So I leaped and hopped and ran towards it, trying to find that source of joy. I asked the child nearest to me—I didn't use words, you understand, but she knew my meaning—and she took me by the hand and brought me to an opening where I was engulfed by light and music. I knew immediately where I was—in the presence of the Lord of Life. I ran and bowed before him and I was singing together with all the other beings around him. He reached out his hand to touch my head. And then, as though he had changed his mind, his hand reached for my hand.

I felt a pull—strong!—to the roots of my being. Even though I loved him and wanted to be with him, I didn't give in to the pull. I wanted to stay in that place of light and dance and joy. But he persisted, holding me tightly, and then I heard a voice say, "Talitha, koumi." The sweet Aramaic words of my home, recognizable words this time, not just meanings. I opened my eyes. I was in my room. I heard my mother's weeping as though it had never stopped. I wanted to comfort her, but my eyes were on the one who was holding me by the hand, refusing to let me go. "Little girl, rise up," he said again. I stood up, still holding onto his hand, my eyes fixed on his. "Why it's *you*," I said, "the Lord of Life." He smiled and put his finger on his lips. "Hush," he said quietly, "It's our secret." He finally let go of my hand and I danced around the room and into the arms of my parents. They quickly pulled me down to the floor with them and asked me to kneel before the Lord of Life. "I already have done so," I started to say, but I suddenly knew that they wouldn't understand.

Outside, a great wailing was rising up. I recognized it as the keening of professional mourners. I looked at my parents. "Who died?" I asked, and my father made a choking sound and hugged me tightly. He started to leave the room, to make them hush, I think, but Jesus—for that was the name his friends called him—was saying something to them. There were three other men in the room. Did I tell

you that? Their names were Simon, James, and John. I could
tell that they were close friends of the Lord of Life. Finally, I
stopped my whirling and dancing and listened. "Give her
something to eat," Jesus told my mother. Only then did she
stop her weeping. Before she could leave the room, in a voice
that sounded sad, Jesus told my parents: "Tell no one of this.
Tell them she was asleep, and now she is awake." I looked up
and saw his eyes. I saw that on this side, the Lord of Life did
look different. He was a man with a dusty cloak and worn-
out sandals, a man who looked tired and even sad. But those
loving eyes were the same. I knew him as I had known him
on the other side—as the Lord of Life.

A year later, when I had turned thirteen, word reached us
that he had been murdered on a cross outside Jerusalem. My
father was in despair because he hadn't known enough about
Jesus' troubles to go to Jerusalem to testify on his behalf. My
mother wept and wailed and was unable to oversee the work
of the house for a whole week. Only I did not weep. "Don't
cry, Abba," I told my father. "They cannot kill the Lord of
Life." My father looked at me for a long time, then he nodded, speechless.

When John the fisherman, the close friend of Jesus who
had also been in my room that day, came by the house a few
weeks later, he told us the astounding story. "Jesus lives
again," he said. "The grave could not hold him. I have seen
him." But he was no longer on the earth, he added, and a
great longing seemed to fill him. "I know where he is," I
said. I too was filled with longing as I remembered the dance
that surrounds the Lord of Life.

Questions to Ponder

1. Was the relationship between your father and you similar to or different from the one between Jairus and his daughter?
2. Jairus's daughter describes a "death" experience. What other firsthand descriptions of death have you heard or read? Do you believe or distrust such descriptions? Why?
3. What details give this story a very human touch and remove it from the supernatural?
4. Does this story comfort you in some way? Why?
5. How has Jesus been the Lord of Life for you?

FOUR

I Am the One Who Touched His Cloak

A STORY TOLD TO GENTILES

Matthew 9:20–22 (9:18–26)
Mark 5:25–34 (5:22–43)
Luke 8:43–48 (8:41–56)

The story of this woman is told by all three of the Synoptic Gospels. In all three this encounter is encircled by the story of Jesus on his way to heal the daughter of Jairus. (Please see previous story.) You may also want to check references to Levitical warnings in Leviticus 15:25 about women in her condition to understand her fear and the courage it took for her to touch Jesus.

I and the little girl Rachel, Jairus's daughter, will be forever bound together. I think I was healed because of her need, and that is part of my story. I have told everyone how I met him on his way to her home; in the telling we are bound together. And bound to him forever.

Mine is not one of the stories our neighbors like to hear because it deals with blood, and blood seems anathema to our people. But since the healer's own blood was spilled from the wounds he suffered on the cross, those who knew him and loved him will talk of blood and be thankful.

You are not our people. You are Gentiles, so you will

need to understand our laws in order to understand my story. My husband left me soon after our marriage, because the bleeding would not stop. He kept quoting the law of Moses to me, while I was bent over crying from the awful cramps and from the shame. I was glad when he left, because then I could hide and be left alone in my misery. Why are women always blamed for what they cannot control? When you find an answer to this question, please come and tell me.

I had been a healthy girl. My father married me off early and from that time on my suffering began. I could not stop the bleeding. So when my husband abandoned me, I was relieved; I thought: Now the misery will stop. But it did not.

My father had left me his money, having no other children, and I started my long search for a cure. First, I visited all the physicians here in Capernaum, then I traveled to Jerusalem and wherever I heard that a physician cured women, but nothing good happened to me. In my travels I drank all kinds of concoctions, distilled so many herbs that I could claim to be a physician myself, offered all kinds of sacrifices as I was ordered, always hoping and then losing hope. I became a wanderer. Twelve years of searching and begging for a cure brought no good results, so I decided to go back to my home, although there was no one there who remembered me or cared for me. I was returning home to die.

Because I did not want people to know of my suffering and shame, I had become a very secretive person. Now that I am cured and know of his sacrifice and of the blood he shed willingly, I cannot remember why I was ever ashamed. But those were the conditions of our law—I was unclean, impure, as long as I bled, and I kept myself hidden as much as possible. (She is a realistic woman who has accepted the radical change in her soul and in her body with equal gratitude.)

I had just entered Capernaum and was walking by the shore when I came upon a great crowd. One can always hide in a crowd, so I thought I would approach and find out what the commotion was all about. About a dozen men, fishermen I thought, were climbing down from the boat and wading ashore. The surprise was that there was a large crowd running towards the boat calling out the name "Jesus, Jesus bar Joseph!" It was an amazing sight, especially for someone like me who had avoided people for so long. "Who is this Jesus?" I asked, daring to speak aloud since there was so much noise, and one little child looked up and said excitedly: "Are you a stranger here? He is the prophet, the great healer. Haven't you heard?" Before I could ask her anything else, her mother had grasped her little hand and had pulled her away toward the prophet.

I tried to see this central figure. Finding courage I did not know I possessed, I pushed forward. I must tell you that once I had been tall and straight, but the constant pain and shame had bent my body, so I walked like an old woman now, although I was only twenty-six years old. I wore dark clothes always. With my stoop and modest colors, I felt hidden among the many colorful women, children, and men around me.

The man Jesus walked quickly through the crowd, followed closely by a group of men that seemed to be his friends. He touched only the children who squeezed through the throng to get close to him. They would pull at his cloak, look up at him, and he would look down, smile, and touch their hair with his palms. When those children moved away, others took their places. The motion of his hands mesmerized me. I was surprised that anyone so much in demand would pause to deal with children. But my surprise was all the greater because he did not seem to mind when they pulled at his cloak. *(She smiles, still delighted with the memory.)*

Suddenly the crowd made way. A man was running through the opening, crying out, "Master, Kyrie, Rabbi!" He seemed an important man, dressed better than the rest, possessing some authority. I heard murmurs around me: "Why it's Jairus, the leader of the synagogue." Together with everyone else I pushed forward to hear the man's pleading. A great "Ah! Look!" escaped like a sigh from the crowd when this man fell and prostrated himself at Jesus' feet. Everyone hushed. Jesus tried to lift him up, but the man remained on his knees.

"Master," he begged, "have mercy. My little daughter is at the point of death. Come and lay your hands on her so that she will be made well and live!"

I started trembling and could not stop. The man's voice pulsated with hope. He reminded me of myself when I was young and the bleeding had first started. How sure I was that I would find a cure! And my heart cried, "Oh, Master, don't take the hope away from him." I couldn't hear what Jesus said, but he must have agreed, because the man was leading the way and Jesus was next to him, walking faster now, and everyone else was following.

And then I knew what I had to do. *(She is still surprised at the memory.)* Where did I find the courage? I think it must have been from the children. "If I can just touch his cloak," I thought, "he will not know it, he will not stop from his mission, and I will be healed." I knew I would not pull at him the way the children did; I would only touch the fringes of his robe. Who would know the difference with so many people around?

Can you begin to understand what determination it took
for me to propel my way through the crowd? I had been a
recluse and there I was pushing and shoving like everyone
else, with one thought only—to get close to him. Instead of
death, life was awaiting me, there on that dusty road, if I
could only touch him!

I inched my way forward. I was close, close. I saw his
strong back, but I bent lower and touched the end of the
cloak that fell behind his shoulder. I just touched it, but I
knew I was whole. My body knew it. The unending hemorrhage had stopped. You'll ask me how I knew. *(She is defiant
now.)* If you had been lame for twelve years and suddenly
you stood up straight, wouldn't you know it? If your head
had hurt for twelve years and suddenly the pain stopped,
wouldn't you know it? I felt this great strength go out of his
body to enter mine. You know how it is when you hit your
elbow and the whole arm tingles? My whole body felt that
kind of energy, and I stood up straight. I pulled back immediately not to annoy him and those close to him. I stayed
behind to savor my healing, this new wondrous feeling in
my body. And then I heard his voice: "Who touched me?"
Everyone stopped and some people laughed aloud. They
looked at each other and shrugged. Jairus was almost jumping with impatience.

One of Jesus' friends answered, and I could hear annoy-
ance in his voice: "Master, look around you. Look at all these
people pressing on you. How can you ask who touched you?
They all did." Jesus' eyes were searching the crowd.
Although my eyes were downcast, I was sure he was looking
straight at me. He said, "I felt power go out of me," and I
knew I had no choice. Jairus was waiting for him to go to his
dying daughter. I was not going to hold him up. I ran forward

(only later did I remember that I had not run in years) and fell at his feet. I was trembling all over. "I touched your cloak, Master," I confessed. "I do not want to delay you from your mission. I have been hemorrhaging for years and all the physicians I consulted failed me. When I saw your compassion to the children who pressed on you and your willingness to go with Jairus, I knew that touching your cloak would heal me. I know, oh Lord, that power went out of you, because I felt it enter me. I am healed. Your power has made me whole." I bent my head to the ground. I felt his voice from above like a balm, a great blessing. "Daughter," he said, "your *faith* has made you whole. Go in peace and be healed from your disease."

He turned towards Jairus and I hugged the words to my bosom. "Daughter," I thought. How long had it been since anyone called me that? I must be young again, I who had felt like an old woman for so long.

I decided to follow him from afar, because now I could not stop thinking of Jairus and his poor little daughter. Rachel and I have talked of this day many times since then. She has told me her story and I have told her mine. We agree that God has blessed both of us in an extraordinary way, allowing us to know him in person, to feel his power go through us, transforming us and making us whole! How could we have been so blessed? We decided together to tell our stories to everyone who would listen.

Sometimes in the late evening, when we sit quietly together and contemplate our lives, I say aloud: "I wonder what my life would be today if your father had not come to beg Jesus for your life. Would I have found the strength to approach him?" Then Rachel, who always calls him "the Lord of Life," says, "I wonder if his power became renewed every time he used it. Don't you think healing you filled him with enough power to bring me back?" And we smile to each other and lift up our hands with thanks to the Lord of Life.

Questions to Ponder

1. How would you answer the question posed in the monologue: "Why are women always blamed for what they cannot control?"
2. Have you known someone who has suffered from a long-term illness or disability? How did it affect his or her faith?
3. How do you explain the fact that this woman and uncounted others have been healed by Jesus while so many appear not to have been healed?
4. In what specific ways have you experienced yourself or witnessed in others the physical, emotional, and spiritual healing of Jesus?

FIVE

An Alabaster Jarful for My Life

A FORGIVEN WOMAN OFFERS HER GRATITUDE AND
REMEMBERS THE ONE WHO CHANGED HER LIFE

Mark 14:3–9
Matthew 26:6–13
Luke 7:36–50
John 11:2
John 8:3–11

*This is the remarkable story of the unnamed woman who comes
to Jesus at a banquet to pour costly nard on his head. Her
prophetic gesture anoints him both as Messiah and for burial.
Mark and Matthew both tell this story; in a different version,
John names the woman. The story in Luke differs from the
others because it comes early in Jesus' ministry instead of close to
his betrayal. In Luke's story the woman is called a sinner and she
washes Jesus' feet with her tears and wipes them with her hair.
This is the version I have followed here.*

*In reading it, I have asked myself: Why is she so grateful?
Has she had a previous encounter with Jesus? I have found
myself going for the answer to the story found only in John
8:3–11, which tells of a woman brought to Jesus to test him and
to make him agree with her planned stoning because of adultery.
The connection I make is based on the loose hair of the woman
who comes to the banquet uninvited—respectable women kept*

their hair covered—on Simon's comment that she is a sinner, and on Jesus' saying that much is forgiven her.

Men went wild when they saw my hair. I wondered sometimes if their wives never loosened their shawls to show them *their* hair. I found men hypocritical but a very reliable source of income. I am not excusing myself in any of this. Listen carefully, please.

It is true that I became who I was because of the men in my family, but the time came when I had a choice. I could have stopped what I was doing, I could have closed my house to men and lived on the fortune I had accumulated, but my life had become a habit not easily broken. I was vain about my looks, despising women who looked down on me and furious at men who came to me in the night but turned their faces aside when they met me in public. I am telling you who I was so that you will know my condition before I met Jesus.

We lived by hypocrisy in Jerusalem, Bethany, and beyond. Women went about their chores pretending to be happy with their lot, when I knew they were seething with resentment inside. They were beasts of burden. They did the fetching and carrying of water, they looked after their broods of children; they did all the cooking, crouching before hot fires. First, they had the even harder job of scrounging around to find wood for the fire that would serve also to heat the room on chilly nights. There were so many unattended children around that even I felt pity on them occasionally.

And the men? Some of them worked hard in the fields and had pity on their children and women. Those I respected and left alone. There were others—with good reputations among men (that is what mattered to them, you see, the opinion of other men) who fulfilled all their duties at the Temple, men who would never think of doing anything so menial as to offer a cup of water to someone dying of thirst on the Sabbath. A few of them I knew intimately. More than anyone else, I knew what hypocrites they were. But they were proud men, and they held the life of the city in their hands.

Do you see the picture I am painting for you? We were all pretending to be something other than what we were inside. I thought I was just doing a job and getting paid for it. Since I had had no one to support me and no hope of ever getting married, what choice did I have? This is how I excused myself. The rest of them? God only knew what was in their hearts, but I could guess rather more accurately than most.

A few of these respectable men were standing outside my door when a client emerged one morning. They left him alone, of course, but they came inside and dragged me out as I was—wearing hardly any clothes. I flailed and screamed at them, but they had a tight hold on my arms as they pulled me through the streets to the square in front of the Temple. Because they had left me alone for many years, I could not guess at first what their purpose was. *(Up to this point she is recounting a story that has bitter memories for her, so she is matter-of-fact. Now her voice changes. The memory is one she cherishes.)*

There was a crowd around the square where a lone man stood speaking in a strong voice that carried: "You, the poor, are blessed by your Father in heaven," he was saying; then immediately, with a kind of smile in his voice, he continued, "I did not come for the righteous, but for sinners." I almost jumped at that. I noticed that the poor ragged urchins and their exhausted mothers had smiles on their faces.

A hush fell on the crowd after a few of them parted with jeers and whistles to let my tormentors and me pass through to stand in front of the rabbi. Then I became truly frightened, because I saw our good citizens bending down to pick up stones.

The rabbi was looking at them instead of at me, as if to give me a chance to cover myself up. One of them let go of my arm, freeing my right hand for a moment. I reached down and pulled the cloth over my shoulders. I lowered my head and waited for what was to come. For the first time in my life, I was deeply ashamed, but I longed to hear again the voice that spoke so encouragingly to the poor and to sinners.

Instead, I heard the voice of my number-one accuser, a man I had known well, who cried in a loud voice, "Rabbi, we caught this woman in the very act of adultery. The law of Moses commands us to stone such women. Now, what do *you* say?" Suddenly I knew that this had very little to do with me; they were trying to trick the rabbi. My fear turned to anger. Here I was again, being used for men's dark purposes. I started to lift my head to spit on my accusers, but something caught my eye down on the ground.

A hand, writing on the sand. Everyone else must have seen it as well, because they stood still and silent for a moment.

Then my accusers' voices, getting more and more shrill, started pelting him with questions. They wanted to know why he did not observe the laws of Moses; they wanted answers about his own person. "Who are you to go against our father Moses?" they kept asking. He remained silent, writing, writing on the sand. I was close enough to see the words, but I could not read them. *(Even now the memory moves her deeply.)*

Then he stood up and faced them. I was so transfixed by him that even I dared to raise my eyes to look at him. He said in a loud voice, "He who is sinless among you, cast the first stone." I started to raise my hands to protect my face, but the stillness arrested me. Through my fingers I gazed at those blazing eyes of his. Nobody lifted an arm. I heard nothing. Only the echo of his words in my ears. Moments passed. I felt hot, stinging tears welling in my eyes—I, who had not wept in years. "I will never be the same again," I whispered to myself. "I don't even care if they kill me now. I finally met a man who is *good.*"

He was down on the ground again, writing, my eyes following the movement of that calloused finger from right to left, from right to left.

After what seemed a long while he straightened up. "Woman," he asked me with great kindness but in a quiet voice that showed he was extremely tired, "where are your accusers?" Only then did I turn to look around me. No one else was there. The square had emptied, the rocks left on the ground, empty accusers of my life.

He continued, "Has no one condemned you then?"

"No one, Lord," I answered, "no one," and the tears ran down my face.

"Neither do I condemn you," he said, and in those words I saw his compassion for my miserable life and felt regret for the first time. I could not move. He searched my eyes, seeing me hesitate; the longing to fall on my knees and worship him was overwhelming. "Go your way," he said, "go, but sin no more."

I will not, my heart cried, I will not!

A woman ran from a doorway and threw a rag to me to cover myself; then she disappeared. How I found my way back home, I cannot remember. *(She pauses and takes a deep breath. Then she resumes the story about herself in a casual way.)*

I'll tell you what I did next. I bought clothes that covered me from top to bottom, especially that hair of mine, so that few could recognize me from my old life. I purchased a beautiful wool cloak, sought out the woman who had shown

compassion by covering my shame, and gave it to her. Then
I started following the rabbi around from afar, for I could no
longer live without his words.

A few months passed, and I kept hearing the rumors. The
same men who had hounded my life were now hounding his.
They were conspiring against him. I wanted to save him, but
I knew I couldn't. So I decided to offer my gratitude to him
and to warn him of danger. I heard that he was in Bethany, in
the home of Simon the Pharisee, a man I had known well. All
the money that was left from my past life I spent on one
thing—an alabaster jar full of nard. I spent three hundred
denarii on it, a year's wages for an ordinary laborer.

Dinner was in progress when I entered Simon's house—
servants coming and going with food, a large group of men
reclining around the loaded table. Jesus' friends were near
him, and a couple of them motioned me to go away. Simon,
the host, was speechless. I saw that he recognized me
instantly. Jesus' back was to me and I could see his tired feet
behind him, feet that had bled with so much walking and
had grown hard from years of travel across the land.

I felt such compassion when I saw his feet that I pulled at
my shawl and loosened my hair. I dared not show my face,
bathed as it was in tears. Instead, I finally did what I had
longed to do the first time I saw him. I knelt down and
washed Jesus' feet with my tears. I had nothing to wipe them
with, only my hair. So I used it as a towel. My heart kept
whispering to him, "You set me free, my Lord, you set me
free. I thank you."

But when I poured the contents of that precious perfume
all over his feet and the room filled with its sweet, strong
aroma, other whispers grew louder. Even his friends seemed
insulted.

"Master, don't you know who she is?" Simon asked with contempt. "She is a sinner."

Jesus did not answer but he turned his body so that he could face me. I bent my head even lower, hesitant to look at his eyes, but I kept washing his feet with my tears that would not stop. In a voice that made the gossip stop, he said. "Simon, you did not wash my feet when I came in tired and dirty from travel. She has bathed them with her tears. You did not offer me the kiss of greeting when you saw me, Simon. She has not stopped kissing my feet. You did not anoint my head as you would have done to an honored guest, but she has anointed my feet with costly nard."

He kept looking at me as he continued, "Yes, Simon, I know who she is. Her sins were great, but her love is greater." Then he stood up and I did the same. I dared to lift my blurred eyes to his. He said aloud for all to hear, "Go in peace, daughter. Your sins are forgiven. Your faith has saved you."

I had only offered him an alabaster jar full of nard for my life, my life. I returned home, cut my hair, sold it to a rich Roman matron, and went to find the poor women I had scorned. I gave them the money to feed their children. The alabaster jar was now filled with his forgiveness.

Questions to Ponder

1. What are the similarities between the role of women in Jesus' time and the role of women in today's society? What are the differences?

2. How does hypocrisy manifest itself in modern culture? In today's church?

3. Note the line ". . . he asked me with great kindness, but in a quiet voice that showed he was extremely tired." Why did the author include that detail in her description

of Jesus? What other impressions of Jesus do you get from this monologue?

4. Have you had a personal experience in which someone defended you? What were the circumstances? How did you respond to that person?

5. Have you previously thought of Jesus as a defender of women? If so, what made that image real to you?

6. Why does the author include the details of the "wool cloak," the cutting of her hair, and the feeding of the poor children?

SIX

Finding My Heart's Desire

MARY OF BETHANY TELLS OF HER
ENCOUNTER WITH JESUS

Luke 10:38–42
John 11:1–45

*The names of Mary and Martha, Jesus' close friends from
Bethany, are found very briefly in Luke; together with their
brother Lazarus, we encounter them again in a more complex,
lengthy, and dramatic story in the Gospel of John.*

All I wanted was to learn to read so that I could know more
about God. From the time I was a tiny girl, I longed to find
out the secrets enclosed in those rolled papyrus treasures I
saw in the synagogue, hidden as I was behind the screen with
the women and other girls. I loved to see the rabbi unroll the
scroll, hold it in hands wide apart from top to bottom,
squinting as he tried to read the magical letters.

My sister Martha thought I was a peculiar little girl. My
brother Lazarus petted me on the hair and smiled his far-
away, lonely smile. "There, there, little one," he'd mumble.
(She smiles at the memory.) The two of them brought me up.
They were both much older than I and, since our parents
were dead, I thought of them as my respected elders. But
that didn't keep me from begging Lazarus to teach me how
to read. He possessed a few of those wondrous rolls of

45

knowledge and kept them hidden. They were his most cherished treasures. I would say, "Lazarus, dear brother, just teach me the letters. That is not too much to ask."

In the evenings, when Martha had cleaned up after the meal and we sat in the lamplight, the three of us together, Lazarus would read to us from the Holy Scriptures. I loved the psalms and the prophet Isaiah most of all. My eyes would fill with tears and my heart would ache with a longing I could not define. Most nights I slipped behind Lazarus and stood looking over his shoulder at the scroll, trying to figure out the shape and sound of each letter. Many times I came very close to succeeding. Then Martha would say, "Come here, little one, and give me a hand in the kitchen." And I would sigh and look longingly at the writing, making a show of it, but then I'd follow her, mumbling the whole time. She laughed and teased me. "Don't be a lazybones," she intoned in her usual good humor. "Mother would not want me to let you grow up knowing nothing about women's duties." "Bah," I would say, "women's duties. They are not for me." And I would toss my hair so it swung defiantly in the lamplight. *(She laughs at the memory of her young self.)*

They were good to me, Lazarus and Martha. I grew up loving both of them, feeling great affection and gratitude. I was smart enough to know that they could easily have let me grow up as a miserable orphan instead of a privileged girl of a good family. *(With the voice of a dreamer.)* It was not their fault that I could not express to them what I felt deep inside. The thought of God, the sight of beauty, and the sound of singing made my heart stir and flutter like the birds that woke me in the early morning. Something deep inside me, unspoken and not understood, made me feel strange. When I grew up to be fifteen, Martha and I seemed much closer in age than when I was only a toddler and she was twelve. She became a sister, then, instead of a mother. She was well past marriageable age, but she was not interested. Martha was happy to keep a home for Lazarus and me.

Our brother also showed no desire to marry. He was content to supervise the tilling of our land and to spend time reading at home. He didn't possess a lightness of spirit. I don't think he wanted to make the effort to find a wife and to go through all the trouble of raising a family. Life didn't have a very strong hold on Lazarus. He seemed to be going through the motions of living, but he was capable of great love and devotion in his quiet, disinterested way.

All this was true and remained so until I happened upon Jesus, the wonderful prophet from Nazareth, the best friend any of us ever made, the best man I ever met, the one who became the center of our circle and of our love for two whole years. I remember how I first saw him and heard him. I was the first one among the three of us. I had planned to go up to Jerusalem with friends, about an hour's walk from Bethany. As we were moving west toward the Mount of Olives, I saw a large crowd of people and, standing on a rise higher than the rest, was their teacher. His wonderful voice carried easily in the spring stillness and, forgetting my friends, I approached in order to listen.

(She is still enthralled by the memory of his words.) He was calling a series of blessings to the people, who seemed utterly enthralled with him. But his blessings were the opposite of what most of us had heard all of our lives. The rich were not being singled out as blessed by God. The happy ones were those who mourned, he was telling them, and judging from their dress most of the people there knew about mourning. "Blessed are you when people hate you," he was telling them, "and when they exclude, revile, and defame you. Rejoice in that day and leap for joy, for surely

your reward is great in heaven; for that is what their ancestors did to the prophets." The ones judged most kindly
were the poor and those who practiced justice.

He was turning most of what I had heard upside down.
"Bless those who curse you," he called out. "Pray for those
who abuse you." He sounded like no one else, except for my
beloved Isaiah. Something about the rabbi's bearing and his
words brought Isaiah vividly to my mind.

Without even stopping to think about what I was doing,
I ran back home, breathless and more excited than I had ever
been. "Martha," I called, "Martha, where is our brother?"

Martha ran to the door. "Why, Mary," she said, "you are
all perspiring; you'll catch a cold. Whatever is the matter,
dear heart?"

"I need to speak to you and Lazarus both," I said. She
sensed that this was not a fancy. I was utterly serious.

"Come," she said immediately. "I think he has just
returned from the high orchard."

I went up to my older brother, kissed him, and said, "My
dear brother and my sister, today I heard the Savior of Israel
speaking on the Mount of Olives."

Something flickered in Lazarus's eyes, and Martha sat
down and fanned her face with her apron. They were both
quiet. They knew I didn't speak lightly about such things. I
told them exactly what I remembered from the electrifying
speech, for I am blessed with an excellent memory. Martha
immediately stood up and said to Lazarus. "Go and find
him, my brother. Bring him here and let us offer him our
hospitality. If he is anything like the good prophets of old, he
has nowhere to lay his head. We have a large, comfortable
home and plenty of food. Go, ask him to come."

Lazarus looked from Martha to me, and I was thinking
at that moment, "My wonderful, good sister. She always

goes to the heart of the matter. And her own heart is as big as any that has housed love." Lazarus chose his best pair of sandals, tied them on his feet, and left us to make his way toward the Mount of Olives. We watched him striding away with a purpose, and I laughed aloud with delight. "Martha, you are a wonder. What can I do to help?" Martha burst out laughing. "You must have heard something wonderful indeed," she said, "for you to offer to help." *(Mary remembers all this with evident gratitude.)*

Together, we shook out the mattresses, lifted the clean linen from among the dried herbs in the special cupboard Lazarus had built, and swept the floor. I was never very good at cooking, so Martha started in the kitchen while I cut flowers to put on the table and the windowsills. We were filled with anticipation. I told Martha how grateful I was that she and Lazarus had accepted without question everything I had told them about the young rabbi.

It was nearly evening when we saw Lazarus returning with our new friend, Jesus. The surprise was that they were not alone. A whole group of Galileans came with them. We had prepared for four and now, all of a sudden, we had fourteen men to feed and probably to put up for the night. Martha ran to the door first. I heard her say, "Master, welcome to our home. Our sister Mary heard you this morning and ran to tell us of the good news you have brought to the poor. We thank God for you. Welcome."

(Life is given meaning by such memories.) There was a wonderful feeling of joy all that evening. We sat in the courtyard, for the weather was sweet and pleasant, and ate, drank, talked, and laughed. What astounded me the most was the transformation in my brother Lazarus. His lethargic, melancholic face became animated for the first time in my memory. He was taken with Jesus as with no other man who had

been in our home, and I was delighted. "Maybe at last," I thought, "Lazarus will fall in love with life." For me, everything that I had thought ever since I was a child was coming together that evening and was making sense. The longing I had had to know God, the pain I felt when I saw the sun setting on the Jerusalem hills painting everything golden red—a pain so akin to longing—the desire I had harbored to learn to read, to know more and more about the meaning of life, were taken seriously by Jesus. I no longer felt strange and different. It was so comforting, so right to be there with him and to listen to him. I sat at his feet, listened, and asked questions.

Poor Martha bustled in and out trying to satisfy the hunger of so many tired men, and there I sat enjoying myself to the fullest. *(Ruefully)* I was not even aware of her. She brought a plateful of fruit to Jesus and I heard her voice say, "Master, won't you tell my sister to get up and help me? Do you not care that she has left me to do all the serving by myself?" Jesus smiled at her and took her hand. He looked at all the dishes Martha had prepared, all the food piled on the table. "Martha," he said, "you are distracted by too many duties. We do not need all this," and he pointed to the results of her continuous work. "One dish would have been enough. Mary has chosen the one thing that she truly needs. It will not be taken from her." I kissed his hand and Martha's and stood up. I no longer felt strange. I knew why it was that longing had filled me from the time I was old enough to recognize it. *(With conviction)* And this was the fulfillment of all my longing. In those hours, Jesus had shown me the face of God, and it was full of love and understanding.

I followed Martha to the kitchen. I put my arms around her and said, "Oh, Martha, now I know why I was born." She petted my back and rocked me back and forth. "Yes," she answered, "yes, I can see that. Go out there and learn all you can. There will be much to learn if we are to serve him." I was filled with joy that she understood me so completely. I ran to Lazarus's special hiding place and pulled out one of the rolls of Isaiah. I knew Lazarus would not scold me. I sat at the master's feet. "Master," I asked, "explain to me this passage about the suffering servant. Why is it that I cannot get it out of my mind?"

(With a kind of resignation) There were many more times that he came to our home, sometimes with his friends, other times to rest, to be with Martha, Lazarus, and me. He was our friend. We loved him and he loved us. Those were the happiest years of my life. I still cannot bear to talk about his death, to know that we were so close and did not know the terror he was undergoing in Jerusalem. It is even difficult for me to talk about seeing him again after his resurrection. I have spent years studying, praying, writing down everything I remember. Yes, I finally learned to read and write. After Lazarus came back to us, he was so filled with joy at being alive that he refused us nothing. So I am spending my time writing down everything I remember about Jesus' words to us. Martha's way of remembering is different from mine, but Jesus taught us that we could choose our way according to our gifts as long as we loved him and one another.

Questions to Ponder
1. Mary is so eager for Martha and Lazarus to know about the Messiah that she runs to tell them. Who first told you about Jesus? What was your response?
2. Do you consider yourself to be more like Mary or more like Martha? Why?

3. Mary is very grateful that her sister understands her "so completely." Why is it so important to feel someone understands us? Who understands you most "completely"? Describe your relationship with that person.
4. Do you agree with Mary that the face of God is a face "full of love and understanding"? If so, how did you come to that conclusion?

SEVEN

Remembering the Human Jesus

MARTHA DESCRIBES THE DAYS IN BETHANY

John 11, 12:1–11

The story of Lazarus is found only in John's Gospel. His description of Martha gives a different impression of the Martha seen briefly in Luke's Gospel, and I have decided to see her only as John sees her. Here I have imagined her as a leader of a church before the great destruction of Jerusalem and the Temple in A.D. 70.

My friends, I will try to answer your questions. (*She listens.*)

"What was it like to see him in the flesh?"

"How much of his nature had we grasped while he was with us?"

You have every right to ask me. In a sense, it is difficult for me to remember. Now that he is the risen Lord, Christós, the anointed of God, it is strange to try to recall the human Jesus of Nazareth. Sometimes I wake up in the middle of the night, I, who together with my sister Mary and my brother Lazarus saw the risen Christ, and I ask myself: Is it possible that God's Holy One sat at my table, ate the food I cooked, laughed with me about my constant efforts to make things as perfect as possible, spent hours talking quietly with Lazarus—is it possible? (*She remains quiet for a while.*)

Then I let my mind drift and I go back to those early, wondrous, and sometimes sad days in Bethany, and every minute comes back etched in clarity and pulsing with his humanity. I thank God again and again, because I am indeed one of God's most blessed women. To have seen Jesus in the flesh and to know him now in his glory—there are not so many of us left who can testify to both of these wonders. The years are passing fast. Soon, we will all be together again— not as before, never as before—but maybe more joyfully. At least that is what he promised, and he always keeps his promises.

(With tenderness) Let me try to go back to those days not only in my memories, but in words, for your sake. My sister Mary has already told you that she was the first among us to hear him. She ran breathless to us and told us that she had heard the Messiah speaking up on the Mount of Olives. Because Mary was an extremely sensitive girl, someone more at home in the land of dreaming and imagining, the realm of the spirit—as we learned to recognize it later—we took her seriously. She was also blessed with a remarkable memory and she quoted the words of Jesus to us. What touched me about those words was his attention to the poor and to the suffering of our people. I had spent much time listening to Lazarus reading to us from the prophets, and I remembered the words of Amos and Micah. I imagined Jesus as one of the homeless prophets of old, because I figured that one who cared for the poor would not be looked upon with favor by the religious authorities. I remembered what our nation had done to the other prophets.

I urged Lazarus to go and bring him to our home, to invite him to eat with us and to spend the night if he had nowhere else to go. Lazarus told me later that Jesus met him as if he had been expecting him. An immediate bond developed between the two men. What I didn't know when I sent Lazarus to him was that, in addition to Jesus, we would be offering hospitality to the group of men he called his disciples, some of whom also became our close friends, especially Simon Peter, our own Kephas, and James and John, the Zebedee brothers.

From that day on our house became a stopping place for them all. Jesus crisscrossed the land several times. I used to wonder about his endurance and his ability to walk mile after mile to bring the news of God's kingdom to all our people. On at least two occasions, he stayed with us for several days to rest. The others went to various relatives and friends and left him alone with us.

Do I need to tell you that those were hours of great joy? *(She smiles to herself.)* And yes, let me admit it, of pride as well. Here was our nation's most famous prophet, staying with us, honoring us with his presence. I often wondered why it was that he liked being with us. I suspected much of it had to do with his feelings about Jerusalem. He loved the city and the Temple, but his visits there always made him sad. Next to his hometown of Nazareth, it was in Jerusalem that he felt most rejected. "Ah, Jerusalem, Jerusalem," I heard him weep once. The weeping broke my heart so I joined him in his grief and tears.

Therefore, he would leave the city to find refuge among us. We accepted him fully as our friend and as our master and our teacher. There was never any question among the three of us that he was sent from God. We offered him love, devotion, good food, a place to wash, to sleep, and to replenish his energies. What did we gain? Everything. He taught us about God and about love. He made us see the close connection between his life and the words of the prophets.

I was the eldest and I worried about Lazarus and Mary.

They were both dreamers, not particularly good in dealing with the problems of daily living, and given to melancholy. But with Jesus, they became animated, asked questions, and laughed a great deal. I felt proud of all three of them.

When Jesus left us, we usually knew where he went. One good thing about the Romans was that they had built fine roads all over Judea, Galilee, Perea, and Caesarea; you would be surprised how frequently people moved around, even then. So we usually had news of Jesus, wherever he went. It often took a few days, but the news eventually reached us. Lazarus had responsibilities with the fields and orchards and for all the servants and their families who needed feeding and looking after, so he rarely mixed with the crowds that followed Jesus. Lazarus did not do well in crowds. I had managed to persuade him that the service we offered to Jesus with our love and our hospitality was just as needed, and that comforted Lazarus.

A large network followed Jesus and loved him—well, look at us now—we already number hundreds among the followers of Jesus since the resurrection!

(Thoughtfully) What troubles me now is that despite all the hours we spent listening to him, we still had not fully grasped that his kingdom was not of this world. How many times he told us. How many examples he laid out before us. All those wondrous parables of his . . . and still, we thought he would redeem Israel here and now. I think only Lazarus understood, but he spoke so little that it was hard to know what he was thinking. I realized only later that death did not frighten him, because he knew that Jesus' kingdom was not of this world. *(She listens to their questions, but for the first time she looks hesitant.)*

Yes, I realize that you are impatient to know more about what happened to Lazarus. Every time I am asked to talk

about this great miracle of the Lord Jesus, I have mixed feelings. I marvel at how accustomed we are to death, yet we are
always surprised and devastated by it. I wonder why it is that
life surprises us even more. Let me start at the beginning.

Jesus had spent a few days with us and had left to go
beyond the Jordan, to Perea. His life was in danger. The religious authorities were very troubled by his words and by the
strength of his personality and had tried to stone him.
Lazarus helped Jesus and his disciples escape to Perea where
they remained until spring. It was during this absence that
Lazarus fell ill. He showed no signs of recovery, despite our
efforts, nursing and pleading with him to hold onto life. I
sent one of our most trusted servants to Perea to ask Jesus to
come. *(She listens and nods.)*

You are right to ask me how I could do such a thing,
knowing that it put Jesus' life in danger. But the love I had
for my brother made me forget the danger to Jesus. Our
human bonds are so close, so close . . .

We sent a message to Jesus, "Lord, he whom you love is
ill." We knew he would understand immediately by the way
we phrased the message that it was urgent. By not giving a
name, we thought it would be safer for Jesus. We didn't want
everyone to know he would be returning to Bethany, so close
to Jerusalem. We never doubted that if Jesus came to him,
Lazarus's sheer desire to live, to be with his friend, would cure
him.

But Jesus did not come. Lazarus died. As is the custom,
we buried him immediately. The burial place was inside a
cave, outside the village borders. Mary and I went into
deep mourning. Because we were well known, many from
Jerusalem came to mourn with us. The house was full again
but it was not joyful.

Four days passed. We remained hidden in the house. I

worried about Mary, who had drifted into her deep melancholy once again. Rumors spread rapidly from village to countryside to town. On the fourth day one of the servants came in and whispered in my ear: "The master is coming. He is even now about three miles from Bethany." I left without saying a word to anyone, not even to Mary. To this day, I don't know what made me so anxious to see him as soon as possible. Lazarus was already dead. I hurried as fast as my legs could take me, being careful not to be seen by the mourners in the house, feeling deeply sad and disappointed and terribly let down. "Why couldn't he have come earlier?" I kept thinking.

When I saw Jesus in the distance, so vibrant and young and radiating goodness, I felt with a stab that had Lazarus seen him like this, he would not have died. For who could die in the presence of life? That is what I thought when I saw him—that he was life. I ran to him while tears streaked my face. "Lord," I called out in place of a greeting. "Ah, if you had been here, my brother would not have died." Irrationally I added, "But even now I know that God will give you whatever you ask of him." What was I expecting? Certainly not what I got. I think that after my outburst, I wanted to assure him that I still believed God was with him.

Jesus, always surprising, looked at me and said, "Martha, your brother will rise again." I felt disoriented. Certainly, I thought, at the last day, and I said so. "I know that he will rise again in the resurrection on the last day." Jesus said the words that made me reel: "I am the resurrection and the life. Those who believe in me, even though they die, will live; and everyone who lives and believes in me will never die. Do you believe this?" He looked at me as if much depended on my answer.

"All I know," I wanted to cry, "all I have ever known is your person, your beloved holy person." I answered aloud: "Yes, Lord, I have always believed that you are the Messiah, the Son of God who is coming to the world." Seeing that this was the right answer, I ran back home to Mary.

(She is making a confession.) I entered her sitting room. Avoiding everyone around, I whispered to her, "Mary, the teacher is here, and he is asking for you." I saw the light come into her eyes again, I saw life return to her limbs as she rose from her couch and ran in the direction I had indicated. I did not regret my words. I followed more slowly, because she needed to see him alone. I saw many of our mourners leave the house to follow her, and I knew that the secret was out. I was filled with the strangest kind of anticipation mingled with fear. Something momentous was about to happen.

I walked to the cave and waited for Jesus, Mary, and the rest of the disciples to approach. I saw immediately that Jesus looked different. He looked as though he had been weeping. At the sight of the tomb, a great sigh escaped him. I was almost unable to bear seeing his great pain at the loss of his friend, so I lowered my eyes. *(She is still troubled by the memory.)* His voice startled me. "Take away the stone," he called out. I went closer to him. Fear had taken over—my fear of death, of the reality of the death, of the stink and the misery and the mystery of it all. Lazarus was dead; we should let him rest in peace. I said to him quietly, almost embarrassed at the thought, "Lord, already there is a stench; he has been dead four days." I had been taught that after the third day the soul left the body. What hope was there?

Jesus turned and blazed those eyes of his at me. "Martha, did I not tell you that if you believe, you will see the glory of God?" I nodded to the servants, and they rolled the stone away from the mouth of the cave. A great hush fell over the crowd. Nobody stirred. We were now in the presence of unknowing. I was trembling so violently that I could hardly stand up. Jesus himself was vibrating with an energy I had never before encountered, even in him. Then a great calm fell over him and he lifted his eyes and arms toward heaven. "Abba," he said in a strong voice, "I thank you for having heard me. I know that you always hear me, but for this crowd here assembled I have called to you so that they may believe that you have sent me." Some in the crowd fell to their knees. The disciples came closer to Jesus. Mary came to me and we held onto each other. Then Jesus' voice again cut through the quiet. His voice was loud and strong, the voice of authority. It almost lifted me up from the ground. "Lazarus," he called out as though cracking the surface of the earth, "Lazarus, come outside."

A huge sigh and a cry emanated from the crowd. We waited. Slowly, like someone in a dream, Lazarus, his feet and hands tied as we had prepared his body, his face wrapped in a white cloth, moved toward the mouth of the cave. I couldn't run to him. Mary was weeping uncontrollably. We waited for Jesus. We wanted to know if this was real. Turning to us, he said in a quieter voice, "Unbind him and let him go."

Mary and I ran together. We didn't want anyone else to touch him. As we unbound his face first, we sensed that Lazarus was laughing. I can't remember much else. There was a great commotion all around. People were running to Jesus and falling at his feet, while Mary and I ministered to our brother. There was no stink in him. His body looked strong and solid and his face had lost all vestiges of melancholy. "Let us rescue the Lord from the crowd," he told us as soon as he could move freely, and together with the other disciples we managed to free him from all those who were clinging to him.

But Jesus could not go home with us. The news of Lazarus's return to life spread even as we were still laughing and crying and touching him to assure ourselves that he would not leave us again. Together with the disciples, we moved to the cover of a copse of trees to discuss what we should do next. John was the one who approached me first. "Martha," he said, as he took my hands in his, "this is such a good thing. But you know what it means, don't you? Those who are jealous and afraid of Jesus will come after him now. Even Lazarus's life may be in danger—not from illness, but from those who fear Jesus and want to silence him. We will try to take Jesus away for as long as he lets us. But I know that the time is coming when we cannot protect him." At that, he laughed ruefully. "How ridiculous this sounds, doesn't it?" he asked me. I nodded in agreement. How does one protect perfect freedom?

I said to John, "There is one thing he insists on: to act in God's holy time. When his time comes, we will be able to do nothing. Until then, we are all in God's hands, aren't we, John?" John smiled. "We forget so easily," he said, "so easily." And Jesus departed with them for a while.

A week before Passover, his time came. All of a sudden, there he was in our home in Bethany. Mary was so happy that she went and spent all her dowry money on a vial full of nard. As we sat around the dinner table, she poured the contents of it on Jesus' feet. The aroma filled the house and we smiled at one another. But Judas was very angry. "Mary," he said, "what nonsense is this? You could have given the money this extravagance cost you to the poor." The other disciples looked at him in horror. "How dare you?" their eyes said, but it was Jesus who spoke. "Leave Mary alone. She doesn't know it, but the perfume is for my burial. Her love will care for the poor also. I will not be with you much longer." There, in the midst of a celebration for Lazarus's new life, we wept. Jesus' hour had come.

You know all the rest. This is what I remember of his earthly stay. But what I focus on now and forever is his face of glory—the Lord who assured us that death cannot defeat him and that by his own death he conquered death for us all. See how bravely all our sisters and brothers who have gone before us have faced the last enemy. Whenever I ask Lazarus about the other side, about what he saw there, he merely smiles. "I cannot talk about it," he says. "All I can tell you is—do not fear. You know the one who loves us."

And that is enough for me.

Questions to Ponder

1. If Jesus asked you, as he did Martha, whether you believe in him as "the resurrection and the life," how would you answer? Why?
2. How would you have reacted if you had been among those who witnessed Lazarus's resurrection? How would you have reacted if you had been his sister Martha?
3. Why did Jesus weep at Lazarus's death when he had the power to raise him from the dead?

EIGHT

There Was No Death in the Man Jesus

<small>PILATE'S WIFE SPEAKS BEFORE A
CHRISTIAN ASSEMBLY IN ROME</small>

Matthew 27:19

This story is found only in Matthew. I have imagined Procla's dream inspired by these words of Dorothy L. Sayers: "There have been incarnate gods a-plenty, and slain-and-resurrected gods not a few; but He is the only God who has a date in history . . . There is no more astonishing collocation of phrases than that which, in the Nicene Creed, sets these two statements flatly side by side: 'Very God of very God . . . He suffered under Pontius Pilate'" (The Man Born to Be King [Grand Rapids, Mich.: Eerdmanns, 1974], p. 5).

We Romans lived by our dreams. Oh, we studied all the omens and read all the signs in the sacrifices and in the flight of birds, but dreams mattered more than even the words of our soothsayers. In this, we resembled the Jews. Why, I knew a noblewoman once who dreamed she would die on the anniversary of Caesar's assassination. She looked healthy and hearty, but as the Ides of March approached, she lost color, sickened, and on the appointed day, she died. I was serious about dreams before but, after her death, I never took my dreams lightly. I made every effort to remember them and even occasionally sent for knowledgeable Jews to interpret them for me. Pontius wouldn't like it if he found out, so I never told him. *(She looks rueful and defiant at the same time.)*

Yes, I know that all of you have heard of Pontius Pilate, my husband. You probably think him a heartless and a vicious man. I have heard the rumors. But I knew him as my husband and as an able administrator. Tiberius would not have left him alone in Judea for ten years had Pontius not been a good administrator. I need to set the stage for those of you who have never been east of the Mediterranean, who have not been exposed to the customs and passions of the people known as the Jews.

I got along well with them. Pontius respected the decree that had given them freedom to worship their God, and I was attracted to this God. My freedwoman Evniki, whose mother was from Galilee, knew much about the Jews and taught me to respect the God of Israel who loved his people. *(But the Roman pride shows through as she continues.)* It was very difficult for a Roman to believe that God had a chosen people other than the Romans—well, it was nearly impossible. I never could bring myself to believe in this Jewish conceit, but I admired their passion for their God, their integrity, and their strict adherence to their laws. *(Her voice drops to a whisper.)* Those of us who knew the evils of the emperors could not take the new cult of emperor worship very seriously. But we were afraid to say so, because it meant death to do so.

Have I set the scene sufficiently for you, Christians of Rome? Don't believe everything you hear about Pontius. Pay attention to what I tell you.

One hot day in Judea, as I was passing by a crowd of Jews gathered around one of their rabbis in the square, near the praetorium, I heard a compelling voice. I asked the porters to

stop my litter on the pretext that I had seen a friend in the distance, and then I raised the curtain a bit and listened. The
voice carried well. It was strong but did not possess the usual
stridency of religious prophets; it pulsated with compassion. I
was riveted by that voice. I had learned enough Aramaic by
then to understand quite a bit of what he was saying. At first,
it seemed ridiculous that God would care for the poor and not
for the rich. *(She is still not quite certain of what she is asking.)*
Wasn't Rome the supreme power in all the earth? But something of what he was saying was touching me in ways that surprised me. "I have come that you might have life, *abundant*
life!" he was saying, and that stopped me cold. My breath
failed me. Abundant life? Here in Judea, for people who were
not Romans? How was that possible, and why did I believe
him when he said it? I shook myself and sensed that the
porters were getting restless. I said to my bodyguard, "Romulus, see what the commotion is. I must report it to my lord
Pontius. Can you have the porters bring me to a rise where I
can see the rabbi's face? He could be a threat to the order that
my husband and Rome have brought to this city," I lied.

Romulus was accustomed to obeying me, so he did as he
was told. Jerusalem is so hilly that it was easy to find myself
higher than the crowd. From this vantage point, I had a clear
view of the Jewish prophet. Suddenly a woman's voice rose
high above all others. "Blessed is the womb that bore you
and blessed are the breasts that nursed you!" she cried, and a
loud murmur of approval rose from the assembly. I saw the
prophet laugh. "Blessed rather are those who hear the word
of God and obey it!" he said in a great warm voice, and then
he turned and looked straight at me. Romulus, immediately
aware of that look, moved quickly, dropped the curtain I had
lifted, and hid me from view. I was shaken to the roots of my
being. *(She is still in awe of that moment.)*

I went home and told Pontius of the encounter near the Temple but did not reveal how it had affected me. He shrugged and dismissed it as a woman's fancy. I tried hard to forget those eyes and the call I had sensed in the prophet's words. I did ask enough questions, however, to learn that his name was Jesus, that he was a Galilean, and that he had a great following all over Judea. I also heard the rumors that he had just brought a man, dead four days, back to life. I tried sacrificing to our household gods that night, but no rest came to my soul.

A week later, the frightful news reached me. Jesus had been arrested. I could not imagine that free spirit, that compelling voice, silenced in the darkness of a prison. I knew Roman prisons. In the night, in the privacy of our room, I asked Pilate to intervene. He shook his head. "Things are moving too fast," he said. "From what I hear, he is already a doomed man." He slept only briefly because soon I heard his slave waking him up with an urgent summons. I fell back into a troubled sleep. That is when I experienced the dream. I have never been the same since.

(This is a memory with a power that never leaves her. She is describing something awesome.) In my dream, the emperor was carried before a huge crowd that seemed to be covering the surface of the earth. A harsh Roman voice was ordering the peoples of the earth to bow down and worship the emperor. The people stood and looked toward the emperor, but nobody moved. Slowly they turned in the other direction, and there stood the prophet Jesus I had seen so briefly a week before. Blood was pouring from his brow and from his hands and feet. There was great sadness and love in his eyes, even though he was being held like a condemned prisoner. All the people, all of humanity covering the earth,

bowed as one and worshiped the wounded prisoner. In the background stood Pontius. Some of the people pointed to him and cried, "He was crucified under Pontius Pilate! He was crucified under Pontius Pilate!" and I woke up with a scream. *(She shivers.)*

I had my slave girl summon Romulus immediately. I told him that I was sending him to the governor with the most important message he would ever receive. Romulus nodded and promised to deliver it verbatim. "Have nothing to do with this righteous man, because I have just suffered terribly in a dream because of him." I made him repeat it and then he rushed to deliver it to Pilate. I waited for him to come back to tell me that Pilate had listened to my message. He knew I never took dreams lightly.

It took a long time for Romulus to return, but the governor's palace walls are like sieves. Rumors fly constantly. So I knew, before any formal report reached me, that the righteous man I had heard only briefly and had seen so vividly in my dream had been sentenced to death and was being led to a cross. When Romulus finally returned that afternoon to tell me of the prophet's death, I felt I was in mourning. Romulus said, "I tried, my lady, but the governor does not care what happens to the Jews, any Jew."

I hid in my rooms and refused to leave them for days. My husband could not understand my grief. I told him, "From now on, my dear Pontius, your name will be linked with the death of this good man. He *is* a king. No, don't try to cover my mouth with your hand! He has nothing to do with the Roman Empire. His kingdom is very different from what we know. In my dream I saw the whole world worshiping him, but even then he looked wounded, he was bleeding. But there was no death in him! Yet, oh Pontius, there was death in *you*." Pontius shrugged again and left my rooms, warning me not to talk to anyone else about this. *(She is silent for a while, remembering, regretting.)*

It took us three more years to leave the place, to leave the Jerusalem I had come to hate. I remained a dutiful wife and never again spoke to Pontius about my terrible dream. All kinds of rumors about the Galilean prophet reached us during our three remaining years in Judea, but Pontius was successful in keeping me away from Jerusalem much of the time—sending me to Aegean resorts for the sake of my fragile health, so there was nothing I could do about the rumors. I could not find any of Jesus' old friends and companions to ask about him.

(The moment has come. This is why she is in front of these Christians.) Here in Rome, with my husband now dead, I listened to the rumors and they brought me to you. I know what some say about you, Christians, but I don't believe them. If you are truly followers of the good man who was crucified in Jerusalem, you cannot be anything but good yourselves. I came to ask you to forgive Pontius, so his soul can find peace. He was not a bad man; he was indifferent—that was his sin. *(She waits. Nothing happens.)*

I am so sorry that the promise of abundant life I heard Jesus giving to his followers did not come to be. Please don't blame my husband for his death. *(She looks startled.)*

Why, what are you doing? Why are you shaking your heads? Why are you weeping and laughing at the same time? Why are you hugging me?

Questions to Ponder

1. Do you think that dream analysis or dream interpretation has any merit? Why or why not?

2. Do you believe God speaks to people in dreams? Why or why not?

3. Pilate's wife says that those "who knew the evils of the emperors could not take the new cult of emperor worship very seriously," but they were "afraid to say so." What kinds of things are people today afraid of saying about their faith? What kinds of things are you afraid to say? Why?

4. In his decision to turn Jesus over to the Jews, was Pilate truly acting on his own or was he merely fulfilling a role that God had already determined for him? If you had been Pilate, what would you have done?

5. After hearing his wife's plea, has your perception of Pilate changed? If so, how? Do you think the perception of her listeners changed?

6. Has there been a time when, as you listened to the gospel, you were "shaken to the roots" of your being, as Pilate's wife was? What happened?

NINE

In the Breaking of the Bread

CLEOPAS'S WIFE CELEBRATES THE REMEMBRANCE OF HOLY COMMUNION WITH NEW CHRISTIANS

Luke 24:13–35
Also read Mark 15:40–16:8 and Luke 24:1–12

Nobody knows who the companion of Cleopas was on the road to Emmaus. Together with recent biblical scholars, especially Dorothy L. Sayers, I think it was his wife, who may be the same "wife of Clopas" mentioned in John 19:25. Only Luke seems in possession of the fragment that tells this evocative resurrection story.

Gnarled, silver-gray olives were surrounding us, and farther uphill climbed the pruned vineyards, just beginning to sprout their green. The air smelled fresh. The shade of the olive trees still held the early coolness of spring, and a bell on the throat of a sheep clanged sweetly nearby. I will remember that scene in all its details until I no longer need memory.

We had stopped to rest, heavy-laden and heavyhearted as we were on that bright, beautiful day, and suddenly the stranger was between us. For a moment I was startled: Where had he come from? The road had looked empty. Then I thought that the olive trees had thick trunks and it was so easy to be hidden by them. "I will walk with you a while," he said, in a calm voice that took all fear away, although we were still surprised at his sudden appearance. I immediately had a feeling that I was in the presence of someone I had known in a dream, but that was too fanciful for me, and I started paying attention.

My husband and I had just descended from the high Jerusalem hills on our way to Emmaus, our home. A week before, we had left our children with my mother and, despite the need of all of us, his followers, to stay together, to support one another in our terrible loss, Cleopas and I felt compelled to return to the children. What if my mother heard of the killing of the master, I wondered? She would fear we had been arrested with him. We needed to go reassure her, but as we left Jerusalem and all our frightened friends behind, our sorrow was not lessened. It became intensified. Cleopas and I discussed every moment of the week that had started out so triumphantly, only to end in the most terrible three days of our lives. We tried to make sense of it, but sense eluded us. *(She recalls their own fears.)*

Why had the beloved master moved into Jerusalem when he knew the authorities were looking for him? Why had he not repudiated Judas when it became quite apparent later that he had known who would betray him? And why, but why, was he condemned? We were troubled by all of these questions, but we kept clinging to the vague hope of today's early morn. I had been one of the witnesses.

We had gone to the tomb, Mary Magdalene, Joanna, Salome, and I, anxious to fulfill our duty, to wash and anoint his blessed body for proper burial. We had watched from afar the night before Sabbath as the good man Joseph of Arimathea and his men had taken the broken body down from the cross. After wrapping it in a clean white linen cloth, they had carried it carefully to Joseph's private tomb, a cave. And we had seen to our terror that guards came and rolled a heavy rock in front of it. We were alone. The men, all of them chosen disciples, had remained hidden. I have never seen such a dispirited group of men before. *(She shakes her head sadly at the memory.)*

We reassured them that no one would harm women who were bent only on a sacred duty to the dead, and we left before dawn to climb to the tomb. As dawn was breaking, we came close to the rock and, feeling our way, we approached the same place where we had stood two days before and watched them bury him. In the early light, instead of seeing the sandy-colored stone, we saw only a dark, gaping hole. We looked at each other, saying nothing. Where were the guards? They were nowhere to be seen.

Mary Magdalene went on ahead and disappeared for a moment through the opening. We saw her backing up suddenly and we ran to her. Something was wrong. What had she seen? She turned to us. "They have taken the Lord," she said as though in a dream, unable to believe what she was saying. "They have taken our Lord." "Who did?" we asked, confused, stuttering. She moved aside. "Look!" she said and started weeping. Two of us entered—we were trembling by then—and waited for our eyes to adjust to the dark. We saw the white linen quite clearly, lying stiff and rolled as if the body had been sucked out of it, and we were filled with awe. What had happened?

The rest of the women started peeking their heads through the opening, afraid to come in any farther. And then, we heard a voice. It was a young, joyful voice, but it took me a long time to remember it as joyful. At that moment all I heard was something so alien that it filled me with fear. The voice said, "Why are you looking for the living among the dead? He is not here." And we looked around. How had we missed him before? A young man dressed in white, so white that it hurt our eyes, appeared beside the tomb as if guarding the empty linen. "Do not be alarmed," he said, but by then we were so frightened, we ran. I think Mary Magdalene was the only one who stayed behind.

My husband was waiting for me. I didn't have the courage to tell him any of this until we had left the city behind us. Only then did I describe to him what we had seen at the tomb. He had been so sad that I feared to give him any false hopes. So I started carefully, telling him of the rolled stone, of Mary's cry—"They have taken away our Lord!"— and he listened, greatly perplexed. But when I told him of the strange young man, his shining quality and his words, "Why are you looking for the living among the dead? He is not here," Cleopas shook his head. I was stunned to see tears in his eyes. "Wife," he said, "your longing makes you see things. You did not see *him*, did you?" he asked, and it was at that moment that we became aware of the stranger between us. *(She shivers slightly.)*

We bent to pick up our bundles, and he asked as we set off again toward Emmaus: "I have watched you looking sad. What are you discussing with such earnestness?"

Cleopas paused a minute and looked sideways at the stranger. "Why, where have you been?" he asked. "Are you such a stranger to Jerusalem that you have not heard what has been happening there during the past few days?" At that moment an unexpected thought went through my head: Just because this is the greatest and saddest event in our lives, does it mean that others feel the same way? I was very surprised at the thought, but it has come to mean something very specific to me since then, as I will explain later.

Instead of answering Cleopas, the stranger asked him another question. "What has been happening in Jerusalem?"

I heard something in his voice that caught my attention. I waited for Cleopas's answer.

"About Jesus of Nazareth," Cleopas started, earnestly now, wanting the stranger to know. "Have you not heard of the great prophet who said words never before uttered, who healed the sick, who did great wonders? Are you not aware that our own leaders handed him over to the Romans who crucified him?"

The stranger did not say anything, so Cleopas continued. "How we had hoped that he would be the one to lead Israel to freedom!"

I jumped in at that point. "It has been three days since they killed him," I said. "And this morning, some of us women went to the tomb and found it empty." I paused and looked at Cleopas, who nodded his encouragement. "We saw a vision," I continued, "a vision of what we think were angels, or one angel—in all that shining light it was difficult to see—and they told us that Jesus is not among the dead; he is alive."

A deep sigh escaped the stranger. "Oh, how foolish you are," he started. "How slow your heart is to believe all that the prophets have told you."

Neither one of us protested. We listened as he talked to us for the rest of the hour while we trudged toward home. "It was necessary for the Messiah to suffer," he explained to us. And then he taught us from the Scriptures. How familiarly he spoke of Moses and Isaiah. What great sense he made of all our history. My burden seemed lifted; later I learned that Cleopas felt the same. We were hanging on the words coming from the stranger's lips. We didn't want him to stop talking.

But there in front of us was the village, its square stone

houses unchanged in the evening light. My heart fluttered at the thought of seeing my children and then, as the stranger lifted his arm in farewell, panic gripped me. "Don't let him go!" I whispered to Cleopas, and he nodded. He ran after our surprising teacher. "Sir," he said. "Look, it is evening. The night is at hand. Please stay with us and break bread with us. My wife's mother is a good cook, and supper will be waiting."

The man smiled and entered our home. We dropped our bundles and I ran to the adjoining room to see my mother and children. In the way of the old and the very young, they were already asleep. Quickly I laid the food on the table. I wanted our guest to keep on talking. His words were like cool, living water. Where had I heard that image before? Questions kept running through my head, but I was too impatient to pay attention to them. Only the present moment mattered.

(Now her voice fills with awe at the memory.) I placed the bread and wine before the stranger. We were still, waiting for him in the sweet evening light. I lit the lamp and, in its soft comforting light, I looked at the man's face. Intense longing squeezed my heart. He stretched out his hand and took the bread. He lifted his eyes heavenward and I started trembling. Then he broke the bread and handed it to us. "Rabboni," I cried, "Rabboni!" Our eyes filled with tears. When they cleared, we saw he was no longer with us.

I threw myself into Cleopas's arms. "Oh husband, husband, all the hours he was with us, why did not our hearts burn within us?"

"O Kyrios!" Cleopas kept saying over and over, "O Kyrios, o Kyrios!"

"Yes," I said, "yes, Cleopas, it *was* the Lord. O Kyrios. It was *our* Lord. How could we not have seen him before? Remember, he chided us about how slow our hearts are to believe. Is that what kept our eyes closed?"

"But now we have seen," Cleopas cried. "Wife, I am going back to tell the good news to the brethren."

"And I am going with you," I insisted.

"But you are tired," he reminded me.

"Tired? I have never felt so refreshed. Let me wake my mother and I will be with you."

My mother was confused. All I could say was, "Stay with the little ones a while longer. We have seen the Lord. He lives." As I was saying the words, I knew that I would spend the rest of my life telling those who did not know of him what I had seen and heard. *(She smiles with conviction.)* For this was not the most important event in our lives only; it was for the whole world to know.

And we walked all night to tell the rest of his disciples that Jesus was made known to us in the breaking of the bread.

Questions to Ponder

1. Have you ever failed to recognize someone you'd known for a while? How did you feel when you finally realized who the person was?
2. There is no hint of ghostliness in this story, not a hint of magic of any kind. What are the details that give realism to the story?
3. What kinds of experiences in your own life have left you as dispirited as Cleopas's wife describes the disciples as being after Jesus' crucifixion?
4. Do you think it's common that people have such a strong longing for something that it causes them to "see things"?

Have you had such an experience? What were the circumstances? How can you tell the difference between realistic hope and foolish optimism?

5. Cleopas's wife wonders whether being slow to believe was what kept their "eyes closed." What kinds of things keep your eyes closed to the presence of the Lord? What kinds of things help you open your eyes to his presence?

TEN

The Visit of the Comforter

PRISCA RECOUNTS TO PAUL
HER OWN ENCOUNTER WITH CHRIST

Acts 2
Acts 18:1–3, 18–19, 24–26
I Corinthians 16:19
Romans 16:3–4
2 Timothy 4:19

*Prisca, also known by the diminutive Priscilla, features promi-
nently in the life of Saint Paul, even though the references are
extremely brief and tantalizing. Her name is coupled with that
of her husband Aquila, but her name precedes his in some references, causing scholars to think that she was the more active of
the two. She was learned and probably not a Jew. Some scholars
consider her the likely writer of the Letter to the Hebrews.*

For you, the vision. For me, the visit of the Comforter. How
do we talk about this to strangers, my brother Paul? You and
I can describe the holy moment to each other, knowing the
other will understand. But can strangers know our meaning?
There are times when I want to hold the memory and mystery to my heart and mind and think on it, but I am com-
manded to go out into the world and share it. Do you never
feel the need to be alone and not have the burden of always
witnessing, always sharing? *(She looks closely at Paul.)* You are
worn out. Your travels have taken their toll on your body

and health. And still, you do not stop a moment. *(She listens to Paul.)* Yes, you did tell me that you spent those three years in Arabia in meditation, prayer, and loneliness. And then you obeyed the Lord's command to go out into the world. You are absolutely right. We must share the good news.

This is how it began for me. Allow me to tell you why I still harbor such deep regret. *(With barely suppressed longing.)* You have had your vision, Paul, and that sustains you. But I, I could have seen him in the flesh. I was close by. And I did *not* see him. Do you understand why my heart aches at times that I missed the great gift of his earthly presence? *(She looks at Paul and smiles.)* Yes, I know, Paul. You do not seem to have this regret. For you the glorified Christ is enough. But for us who were in Galilee at the same time, it is different. Jesus of Nazareth should have been my teacher as he was to Peter and to John and to James. He *should* have been. How could I have missed him?

Yes, let me tell you how it was from the beginning. I was quite young then. My mother was widowed and her good friend Joanna asked her to come to the palace in Tiberias to help her husband Chuza with all the translations and the interpretation of different languages. My mother was Greek as I have told you, and my Jewish father—who was really an apostate—had not kept her from her studies. She knew Greek and Latin and Aramaic and could understand several of the languages of those who wrote reports for the palace. And Chuza, as Herod's scribe, needed many helpers. Both my mother and I had a gift for languages, and we were grateful to find a source of income now that Father was dead and we were alone in the world.

We knew that Joanna disappeared for weeks at a time, and we knew that she was a follower of a prophet, but my

Greek mother was not really interested in religions and cults, as she called them, and we did not discuss Joanna's other activities with her. It was enough that she was kind to us. Chuza was a considerate employer, so we kept to ourselves. Jews did not like to come to Tiberias because of Herod and his desecration of the gravesites, so we heard very little of what went on outside the palace, on the side of the lake where Capernaum throbbed with the words and presence of Jesus, as I heard later.

I am trying to tell you what I was before, so that you can understand who I am now. We had been there for some time when we noticed that Joanna had returned to the palace from the last Passover observance a different woman from the one who had left. She was no longer content to live inside the palace walls, and she urged us to move to her home in the town, something we accepted with much pleasure. Life in the palace had become monotonous and for me, as a young girl, at times it was dangerous. So we lived in one room in Joanna's house by the sea, and Chuza went to the palace during the day to fulfill his duties to Herod. When he needed work from us, he was able to bring it home, so that was much easier. Joanna was in a strange place between grief and joy, a woman who seemed to be expecting something wonderful to happen. Instead of keeping to herself, she made every effort to speak to me, to tell me of her beloved prophet who had been murdered during the Passover in Jerusalem. She had given up on my mother, who was "not interested in prophets," as she put it.

Joanna started telling me stories about every encounter she had had with Jesus. She remembered his words with a vividness that surprised me, and I would make notes on pieces of papyrus I had saved that had been torn off and discarded from palace scrolls. The more I heard about the words of Jesus, the more intrigued I became. I found that I could not stay away from Joanna. I wanted to hear more and more. Every parable of the kingdom that she recounted went straight to my heart and I thought about it the rest of the day and into the night. *(She is now excited.)* She told me how Jesus avoided signs and wonders and how the longing of the people to see more and more of them troubled him. Although he warned them again and again that this was not the way to the kingdom, he could not resist healing those who were sick and maimed; it was as if illness could not persist in his presence. Whenever there was love and faith in those who pleaded with him, he responded with forgiveness and the gift of wholeness.

I was so filled with his words that I could think only of him all day long. I started feeling this intense longing to see him, not to be left out of his kingdom, which I already understood was not of this world. The days were filled with Joanna's words and memories. One day she took me to meet Kephas, our brother Peter, and he also told me some of the same stories—but many of them showed how blind Jesus' disciples had been during his lifetime, and that surprised me. Peter kept assuring me that I could also know Jesus, even though he was no longer on the earth.

The Feast of Weeks was approaching, fifty days after Passover, and Joanna invited me to go to Jerusalem for the observance. My mother had no objections, so we made the preparations for the trip. A large number of us were traveling from Galilee, and it was very festive and joyful. I realize now that all the Galilean friends of Jesus had decided the time had come to be open about him, and they could no longer stay in their beloved Galilee. Everyone in the group had known the living Jesus, and I would go from one to the other trying to hear everything each one remembered. I found John's memories similar to Peter's, but his choice of words was different. Although these two were Jesus' closest friends, they remembered him with different emotion. *(She is a learned woman and looks at everything with an analytical mind.)* I thought then how difficult it would be for the story of Jesus to be told in such a way that all the listeners would accept it. And I recognized somewhere in my young mind that this was the living reality—a person with such power as Jesus had demonstrated would leave different imprints on all he touched, according to each person's disposition and personality. It was a new thought and it intrigued me. But how long could memories last? Why were all of the people who had loved Jesus not mourning him but speaking of him with such joy? When I asked this question of Joanna, she smiled mysteriously and said, "This is something you will be told at the right time."

Before entering Jerusalem, we spent one night in Bethany, in the home of Martha, Mary, and Lazarus, Jesus' very close friends. *(The memory is very sweet for this practical woman.)* I was in awe. The men went with their brother Lazarus to sit outside under the stars to reminisce, and we women stayed inside. The soft light of the lamps lit the faces that were becoming dear to me as they told me wonderful stories. I listened, enthralled. I listened with all my being. Martha described moments she remembered of Jesus' visits in this very home, and Mary showed an astounding ability to recount his words. There was another woman there, Mary of Magdala, Joanna's good friend. I sensed that there was something they were all waiting to recall together in my hearing.

"She was the first to see the Lord after his death," Joanna

said to me. I looked at her, startled. This was something new. "What do you mean?" I asked her. "Has she seen a vision?"

Mary of Bethany spoke up. "Why, Joanna, have you not told Priscilla of the Lord's appearances?"

Joanna smiled. "I thought it would be more convincing if it came from the chief eyewitness among us."

Mary the Magdalene spoke for the first time. "Priscilla, do you know what happened during the Passover?" I nodded, unable to utter the words. How could I speak of Jesus' murder in front of these women who had witnessed it?

"We were there when they crucified him," she continued in a quiet voice. "And we were at the tomb on the third day."

Martha and Mary shook their heads with regret. "But not we," Martha said. "In this we failed him."

"But you had not even heard of his death yet," Joanna said. "How could you have been there?"

Tears filled Mary's eyes, Mary of Bethany, that is. "We should have been at the foot of the cross also," she said. Her sister put an arm around her.

"This is no time for regrets," Mary of Magdala said sternly. "We are here to tell Priscilla what happened. She is the one who will carry the good news of the resurrection to places none of us will ever visit. With her youth, her languages, and her passion, she will go where the story must be told."

(The weight of that is still on her mind.) I was speechless and had started trembling. Who did they think I was? And what did she mean by resurrection? I clutched Joanna's sleeve and waited. All the women nodded and turned toward the Magdalene. She closed her eyes for a moment and then she gave me a radiant smile.

"We discovered the empty tomb first," she said. "We

stood near him at the cross and we watched as they buried him. We visited the tomb after the Sabbath to minister to his body but his body was not in the tomb. And the Lord blessed us with the assurance of his resurrection."

"Resurrection," I repeated, trying to remember what I had heard of the teaching of the Pharisees. "Isn't that to be only on the last day?"

"This is *the Lord's* resurrection we are talking about," Mary said. The others nodded, their faces lit with wonder. "The Lord Jesus, our beloved Rabboni, could not be held by the grave. Sometime after the Sabbath ended, in the middle of the night, his bonds were loosened and he left the tomb. We thought someone had taken his body away, but the truth is that he was no longer dead."

"But how do you know?" I stammered.

"He appeared to me in the garden later that morning, and he called me by name," Mary of Magdala said. Great tears ran down her cheeks although her face was lit with joy. "And he asked me to tell his friends, his brothers and sisters as he called them, that he was alive."

"Did you recognize him?" I asked, "Did you know him as before?"

Mary shook her head thoughtfully. "Only when he called me by name did I know him," she said softly. "There was something about him that was different; he was younger and more distant. But his voice was the same, and I could see the nail wounds on his hands and feet. His love surrounded me more palpably than before, but I couldn't quite touch him."

All of us remained quiet for a long while, lost in our thoughts. I found it difficult to break the silence, but I had to know.

"Anyone else among you?" I asked—and they knew my

meaning. They all nodded. "He came to reassure us," Martha said simply. "We had loved him so much. This was his home whenever he needed it. He came to reassure us," and she touched her sister's hand. "Otherwise, we could not have born our absence when he needed us," Mary added. "We had waited for him to return that Thursday night, but he never came back. It was three days later that we learned of his crucifixion and burial. By that time, the news was breaking that he had been seen by some of the disciples. And he visited us also to reassure us. Blessed be his name."

I was breathless. I was torn between longing and a strong skepticism. I had read many of the Greek and Latin writers, and resurrection was much to accept. I could love him as a teacher, as a prophet, but this was too much. The women looked at me expectantly, but all I could do was ask permission to think on these things.

The next day we left for Jerusalem. Everyone was kind to me, and they did not press me in any way. We gathered in a large room in the home of a man named Nicodemus. He had been an admirer of the Lord Jesus but had not been open about it. I learned from the women that he had helped Joseph of Arimathea, another secret follower, in the burial of Jesus' body.

There were many people in the room. For the first time I saw the Lord's mother. I went near her and kissed her hand, and she laid it briefly on my head and smiled. Then I sat between Mary Magdalene and Joanna and waited with them. I did not know for whom. When I asked Mary, she said, "He promised us a Comforter."

Peter stood up and read from Isaiah and then John offered a prayer. I had never been to the synagogue, but I imagined this was customary. There was a great sense of anticipation in the room. A deep quiet followed the readings and the prayers, but it was not uncomfortable. *(Her eyes fill with the image of the moment.)* Then something like a susurration started; it reminded me of the sound of the wind coming from the opposite side of the lake. It gathered speed and volume and the doors of the room opened wide. Everyone stood up and looked around. I saw a glow on their faces, a light that moved and was touching everyone. It was like the glow of a fire that burned but did not consume. I have tried for years to find the words to describe what I saw, but it is nearly impossible. Like your experience as you approached Damascus that day, Paul. It is not possible to find words to describe something that enters our realm from the other side, from the source of reality, from the Spirit to the senses. All I know is that soon we were laughing and praying together, and someone started a song. Peter and John were the first to leave the room and everyone followed.

The sound had attracted people from the crowded city. I heard languages all around me. Some were new to me, but I could understand what they were asking. "Are these people drunk?" they asked. I answered, "No, not drunk. It is only nine in the morning. They are joyful." And I realized just as suddenly that I was changed. The skepticism of the night before had left me and I was filled with the greatest assurance that the living Lord Jesus was just as present to me as he was to those who had known him in the flesh.

I had become separated from the rest of the women and tried to find them in the huge crowd, but everyone was moving toward the portico of the Temple and I followed. It was during that surge that I first met my husband-to-be Aquila, but that is another story. We stood together to hear our brother Peter address the crowd, and we were together when we were baptized in the faith. The rest, of course, you know already.

(Eagerly) Do you think anyone else can understand what happened on the day of Pentecost? Since then, I have been aware of the presence of the Comforter in all our troubles and our travels, and in the ordinary daily lives we lead. I am sure that the Holy Spirit brought you to us here in Corinth, Paul, the same Spirit that gave me the assurance of Christ's living presence. Thanks be to God.

Questions to Ponder
1. Do you think it would have been easier to be a believer if you had known Jesus during his earthly life? Why or why not?
2. Prisca describes feeling "torn between longing and a strong skepticism" after she heard the account of Jesus' resurrection. Was it easy or difficult for you to believe the resurrection story when you first heard it? Why? Do you still feel the same way? If not, what has changed?
3. Prisca says she is "aware of the presence of the Comforter in all our troubles and our trials, and in the ordinary daily lives we lead." Are you comfortable with the idea of the Holy Spirit's active presence, or does talk of being "born again in the Spirit" put you off? Why?
4. Do you think people like Prisca and Paul and their friends could have survived in our memories and tradition as they were establishing churches had not the Holy Spirit been a reality for them?

ELEVEN

Walking in the Light as a Servant of Christ

Phoebe Introduces Herself to a New Family of Believers

Romans 16:1–2

Only two verses mention her, but volumes have been written about her. Phoebe is the first deacon named in the New Testament. Paul commends her highly to the believers in Rome and entrusts her with his letter, something that does away with our prejudices about Paul concerning women, in my opinion. Kenchreae is the eastern port of Corinth, about eight miles from the city. Excavations have shown the remains of a beautiful early Christian church there.

One day a woman walked into my workroom in Corinth and changed my life. Doesn't that sound strange and familiar at the same time? We wake up one morning thinking the day will be the same as yesterday, content and comfortable with our routine, and then a chance encounter turns everything upside down. But we never suspected it when we greeted the light of day. Yet, is it a chance encounter? Is anything controlled by chance in our lives? I discuss these questions regularly with brother Paul and my sister Prisca when we visit together.

My name is Phoebe. I was named by my parents for

Phoebus Apollo, because they both worshiped the Greek
god of light and music and poetry. They taught me to love
beauty, and I thank them for that and for my sunny name. I
started to weave very early in my life. My parents encouraged
me in the craft because I was creating lovely designs on the
cloth I wove on my large loom. So when I was widowed
quite early, I was able to continue supporting myself. My
workshop in Corinth had become very popular with the
Romans, since the men were vain about their togas and the
women loved cloaks with elegant designs. I was very comfortable living with my two slave girls, both clever at the
loom, and one male slave who served as caretaker. Although
I was rather well-to-do, I despised the custom of the Romans
who surrounded themselves with dozens of slaves. But I will
tell you more about them in a minute.

That was my life when a woman named Prisca walked
into my front workroom one day and asked me to weave a
warm cloak for someone who traveled extensively. She was
tall for a Jewish woman, but I soon learned she was half
Greek and well educated, more like a Greek male than a Jewish woman. There was something instantly appealing about
her, something strong and calm, and I liked her immediately.

She looked at me with a kind of amusement in her eyes,
as if she had known me in the past, and described what she
wanted—a dark-colored, warm wool cloak that would give
protection to her friend on his many and difficult travels.
She wanted something simple, no adornments, she said. I
quoted her a price. She agreed to it and asked if she could
come back to see the progress of the weaving. I invited her to
come as often as possible, something I did not do with
everybody who ordered cloaks. She smiled warmly and left.
(She is very comfortable telling her story.)

I had just dyed the wool and had spun it into a thick,

sturdy yarn when she returned. It was three days later.
"Phoebe," she said, soon after inspecting the brown yarn, "I
am pleased to see that you don't have many idols in your
workroom." I laughed. "You haven't been inside the house," I
said, surprised and amused that she would bring up such a
subject. There was only a small idol of the god Apollo in the
front workroom, but in the atrium of the house were the
usual lares and penates, the household idols of Roman homes
that even we Greeks had adopted. It was usual and proper to
offer a small sacrifice to the household gods every day—then
we forgot them and went about our daily business.

Nobody had asked me about the idols before, and I was
intrigued. I invited her inside the house, which was behind
the shop. She looked at the atrium with lively interest and
moved close to my small idols, chosen as protectors of the
weavers. There was a small carving of Athena and one of
Hestia. Prisca stood before them thoughtfully, and I
invited her to sit and take some wine and water with me.
She agreed.

I could not resist asking, "Why are you interested in my
gods?"

"I am interested in people's *beliefs*," she answered without hesitation. She didn't offer any other explanation.

We drank our cooled wine and made small talk about life
in Corinth. She told me they had been living in Rome, she
and her husband Aquila, but things had become difficult for
Jews there and they had chosen to move to Corinth. "We are
leatherworkers for tents," she explained. "I draw the designs
and my husband cuts the leather for the tent bindings and
for cushions and other furnishing that go into tents and car-
riages. Recently we have accepted the assistance of a new
friend. He is the one who needs the warm cloak."

I waited for more, but she was the kind of woman who

could be silent without needing to make idle conversation. She seemed so calm and in control that I wanted to know more about her. I decided to take the plunge, although I was not naturally a curious person.

"Prisca," I started, and she gave me her full attention. "Are you of the Jewish faith?" "Yes," she answered immediately, "though, like you, I was brought up with much knowledge of the ancient religion of Greece and of the Roman cults. I am Jewish on my father's side but Greek on my mother's side of the family." She paused.

I felt that she wanted to say more, and I encouraged her. "What is your status now?" I asked, and thought: I am crossing a line. She smiled that radiant smile of hers that filled her eyes with light. "And now," she said, "I walk in the light." I felt something tingle in my spine, like a premonition, a knowledge I had had from infancy and had just discovered. I stared at her. Finally, I found the words: "Prisca, I was just thinking that your eyes fill with light when you smile, and you spoke of light. I am not as superstitious as most Greeks, but I felt a strange thrill when you spoke of walking in the light. Apollo is the god of light, but I have never known this state . . ." I stopped because I became confused.

She put down her glass of wine and entered a stillness I later came to know well. "Phoebe," she said, looking at me as though she was searching my soul, "there was a man who recently lived in Palestine. He called his followers children of the light. He called himself the Light of the World. And nothing in his short life, in his words and his actions, disputed this claim."

I felt the breath catch in my throat. I had so many questions, but I asked the most obvious. "His *short* life? Is he dead?"

"He was put to death like a common criminal when he was barely thirty-three. He was crucified by the Romans with the agreement and cooperation of the religious authorities of my people."

"But why, why? If he was the kind of man you describe, why would they do this?"

"The only analogy I have, and it is a limited one, is with your own Socrates. Your philosopher who was put to death for telling the truth as he saw it, who chose to die for the truth rather than give in to those who were afraid of it."

I was hooked. "Tell me more," I said, and that is how my life changed.

The stories I heard about the man Jesus became a lifeline for me. I begged Prisca to tell me all about him. What I loved most about her stories was Jesus' desire to help the poor, to share their lives. I have never known an important Greek who would do this, and certainly never a Roman. Only the rich, the victorious, and the famous mattered in our society in Corinth. The terrible custom of exposing unwanted babies still occurred among the poor citizens of Corinth. They left their babies outside to die because they could not support them. I used to think I was a fool to care about what happened to needy people, but here was a marvelous teacher who shared my concern and who showed that I was not a fool. How wonderful, I thought, and my heart filled with longing to know more about this Jesus, to see his face. I devoured the stories Prisca told me. I wept repeatedly as she recounted his arrest and the horror of the crucifixion. The resurrection story, I kept thinking, was too good to be true. How I longed for it, and how difficult it was to believe it.

And then the day came when Prisca brought Paul, "their

new assistant," to my workroom, on the pretense of trying on the cloak I had completed. I had heard a great deal about him by then, but I was not interested in him; I wanted to hear only about Jesus. So when Paul, short, slender, and rather unassuming, entered with the handsome Prisca, I barely lifted my head from doing some last-minute stitching on his cloak. He came and stood near me, watching my hands at work. "So this is the remarkable weaver of cloaks," he said quietly. "Remarkable?" I asked just to make conversation.

"Prisca thinks highly of your work," he said as I lifted the cloak and stood up. "Would you like to try it on?" I asked and handed it to him. As he was draping it around his shoulders, he said with a smile, "It is very beautiful, Phoebe. I ruined my only cloak climbing your steep mountains and sleeping on the hard ground as I made my way from Berea to the coast and then to Athens and Corinth. This will last me a long, long time."

I said nothing. I was always pleased when my work was appreciated. "For some reason," he continued, "I am reminded of a story the Lord Jesus liked to tell to those who worried too much about their possessions. 'He who has two cloaks should give one to the poor,' Jesus said," and at that, Paul looked me full in the eyes.

"What a wonderful saying," I cried immediately, deeply touched. "Did you know the Lord Jesus?"

"I now know the Lord Jesus," he answered. "I have seen him."

Bewildered, I looked from Paul to Prisca. She only smiled and seemed to be waiting for something. I invited them to accompany me into the living area of my house, and they followed me. Wordless now, I pointed to the seats, and they obeyed. Paul started his story as if he knew I longed to hear it. "I am not one of the first disciples of Jesus," he explained. "I was not living in Palestine during those years and had not heard of Jesus until after his death. When I did, it was with the most terrible misunderstanding. I decided that his followers had abandoned true adherence to Jewish law and I set out to bring havoc upon them. I did. But on the way to more persecution, I was stopped. Mercy and loving-kindness stopped me." He paused, obviously from deep emotion, and both Prisca and I remained quiet. I thought he must have told his story before. I wondered why it still brought such strong feelings to the surface. "I was thrown from the mule I was riding by a light so bright that it blinded me for three whole days. And I heard the voice of Jesus asking me, 'Why do you persecute me?'"

"How . . . how did you know it was his voice?" I stammered.

"I asked him, 'Who are you, Lord?' and he told me, 'I am Jesus whom you are persecuting.' I am convinced he wanted me to know that I was not only persecuting his followers, I was persecuting *him*. And with that knowledge my life changed."

He remained quiet as if reliving that crucial moment of his life. I no longer saw him as nondescript. There was light emanating from him as well. I had never seen such strength of character written on a face. I knew that I was in the presence of truth. I approached him and began to kneel, but he stopped me and stood up to face me. *(She is now under strong emotion as she remembers.)*

"Phoebe," he said, "I have a strong conviction that you want to show me someone." I was so startled that I grabbed his hand. "Yes," I said, "yes, but how did you know?"

"The Lord reveals some things to me," he said simply, so I led him and Prisca to one of the rooms in the back of the house. My male slave had a daughter who had given birth and who now hovered on the threshold between life and death. I had been much concerned with mother and child and had managed to find a nurse for the infant so that she would not die with her mother. My slave Aristos was a good and faithful man and I wanted desperately to help him in his distress.

I entered the small room where the girl Erato lay and asked her father if my guests could enter. "He is a man sent from God," I whispered to him, and Aristos nodded. Paul approached the bed where the unconscious girl lay in the fever that burned her. "Her name?" he asked the father. Aristos whispered, "Erato. Her mother also died at childbirth."

"She will not die," Paul said simply and knelt by the bed. He took the girl's hand in his own, then lifted up his eyes and looked at Prisca. She immediately knelt and took the girl's other hand into hers. Then Paul started praying. I could not hear the words, but there was no question that he was praying to someone he could see. The prayer lasted one hour. I was reeling on my feet and had sent the poor father outside to get some air, but I refused to move. I wanted to be in the presence of the Spirit that engulfed Paul and Prisca and the feverish girl on the bed. She was responding. A moan escaped her, and then large beads of sweat covered her forehead. When Paul stood up, he looked utterly exhausted. "Wash her and give her something to eat," he told me. Prisca and I did exactly as he had ordered.

When I returned to the atrium, I told Paul, "Now I am ready to be baptized, my brother Paul." *(She smiles warmly as she tells of a decision she has never regretted.)*

"Do you believe that Jesus is the Son of God?" he asked me. I answered, "Yes, I have seen him on your face. I know now that he lives."

"You have seen him because you believe," Paul responded, and from that moment we have worked together. *(Now she looks at her new friends, needy people who are enthralled by her story.)*

I am here in Kenchreae because he asked me to look after you in his absence. With your sailor husbands and fathers out to sea, who will comfort you and help you? Jesus asks us to look after one another. So here I am, together with my former slaves, now freed men and women who have been baptized in the Lord. I know you call me your *prostates*, and so I am—the protector appointed by God and by our brother Paul. But what I really am is a *deacon*—that is the word Paul uses for me—and in that I glory. Here I stand, your deacon, your servant Phoebe, who has been blessed with the call to service.

Questions to Ponder
1. Describe a time in your life when everything was suddenly turned upside down. How did you feel during that time? What kinds of things did you do to cope until your life became stabilized again?
2. Are "chance encounters" really by chance, as Phoebe asks? How much of an active role do you believe God plays in bringing people together?
3. When and how did you first hear the gospel story? Have you ever had an opportunity to share your faith story with someone else, as Prisca and Paul did with Phoebe? If so, what were the circumstances?
4. What is the difference between a "servant" and a "deacon"?

If you have ever been a deacon (or if you are an ordained deacon) in a church, describe the activities you performed and the effect they had on your spiritual life.

5. What does the phrase "walking in the light" mean to you?

TWELVE

Seeing the Face of Christ in Those of the Redeemed

A YOUNG WOMAN ENCOURAGES BELIEVERS
IN THESSAONIKI DURING THE TIME
OF NERO'S PERSECUTION OF CHRISTIANS

1 Thessalonians
Acts 17:1–15, 19:21–22, 20:1–4

The narrator is an imaginary person. It is obvious from Paul's first letter to the Thessalonians that he became very attached to them. There is wonderful warmth and love in his letter. Luke tells us in the Acts of the Apostles that there were many women who feared God and accepted the good news of Jesus, so a woman who met Jesus through Paul is very probable. The city can point to no specific place of Paul's visit, but the locale of the ancient city is still the same and the description offered in the monologue must be what the first Christians saw. Paul visited the churches he founded in Macedonia at least twice. Because Thessaloniki, the capital of ancient Macedonia in Greece, is my hometown, the first believers there, especially the women and the children, have always fascinated me. This is my tribute to them.

Last night we received the sad news that our brother Paul is dead. It took a long time for the terrible suspicion we harbored for months to be confirmed, but now we can no longer have any hope. The messenger, our own Aristarchos, arrived worn and bedraggled last night after harrowing travels across the Adriatic, our western mountain roads, and the Via Egnatia. He entered our home first and told all of us assembled there of Paul's final days. That Nero is demented nobody doubts, but now we know that his madness has turned on us, the Christians. After hearing Aristarchos's story, we who have been Paul's disciples from the beginning decided among ourselves not to give in to fear. We will continue as before, for this is what Paul asked of us. I came here to this young *ekklesia* on the mountain to urge you to have courage. Remembering his love for us and his joy in our steadfastness, I know I am speaking on Paul's behalf also. *(She listens to questions.)*

Yes, my dear sisters and brothers, I know that he expected the *Parousia* in his own lifetime. It did not happen. Paul's early conviction of our Lord's imminent return altered through the years. For this reason, and many others that will become clear, I climbed the hill this morning. I needed time to think on what has happened and longed to see the city again from this high vantage point. I have always loved Thessaloniki and have never wanted to live anywhere else. To see the Thermaic Gulf from this hill and the sun's rays bursting on its waters, to be filled with awe at the majesty of Olympos and his snowy heights so clear across the glistening bay, to see the dark green of the cypresses against the blue of the sky and smell the thyme and chamomile on the dry earth—this is one of life's greatest gifts. How can one doubt God's hand of creative love when so much beauty surrounds us?

As I was climbing uphill, I thought on these things and was grateful that Paul had a chance to see this earthly loveliness once. I remembered what I was before Paul's visit here fifteen years ago. I was very young then and given to easy worship of beauty. I would look at the magnificent shape of our bay, at the River Axios as it wound its way from the north to touch the waters of the sea, and I would contemplate the heights of Mount Olympos. I know that our people here in Thessaloniki have believed that gods dwell on those formidable crags. It would be easy to do so. The greatness of the mountain range and the wonder of the sunsets over the bay could fill a mind with thoughts of the divine. We have every testimony that the ancients did so. Look at all the shrines to Zeus around the city, and the furor with which our faith has been met by his adherents.

But it was the *character* of those gods that made me suspicious. Even as a child I found it hard to believe that serious thinkers like our Greek ancestors could ever have worshiped gods so fickle, so capricious, and so indifferent. But try to question the sacrifices and the wealth spent on the temples and all their ritual, and you run into a conflict with the merchants of the city and with the greed of everyone associated with pagan idols. One or two among you may remember what happened when Paul first brought us the good news of a God who cares for us and not for showy sacrifices, golden idols, or marble statues. It was not an easy time for him.

Some of our brothers and sisters came to us from the synagogue where they had already learned of the one God. But others, like me, heard the good news in the streets of the city. I remember walking with my parents by the sea on a lovely evening and seeing a large crowd gathered in the square adjoining the quay. We approached and saw a foreign man on the podium speaking to those assembled. He spoke of a God he called "Father" and of the Son of the Father, Jesus the Christ. I was immediately attracted to the story of a loving

God who entered humanity in our form to share our lot and to bring an end to our confusion. My father, who never could resist a good story, invited the strangers to take a meal with us. Jason, their host, came with Paul, Silvanus, and Timotheos, and we became fast friends. That meal in our house was the beginning of continued fellowship and animated conversations.

Because of my youth and precocious gifts, I was chosen to tell our guests the history of our city. I remember how they stood me up on one of the stools and how proud my mother looked as I started with Alexandros and his exploits. My father turned to Paul and smiled. "This must be why all of you from the eastern countries speak such beautiful Greek." Paul nodded, "Even Alexandros's work on the expansion of the language was ordained by God," he said simply, and that was that.

I was only ten years old, so all the adults had this sweet, indulgent expression on their faces as I told them how the name of the city came to be. "Alexandros's father was Philippos of Macedon," I quoted from my tutor's lessons, "and he married many wives. When he returned from a victory over Thessaly, south of here, he discovered that one of his wives had given birth to a little girl. He promptly named her 'Victory over Thessaly'—Thessaloniki." I waited for them to remark on the name, and then I continued. "Kassandros, one of Alexandros's generals, married Thessaloniki and named this city after her."

My father looked at Paul. "This is where the story runs into difficulties," he explained. "In order to populate this city by the water, Kassandros emptied twenty-six surrounding villages. I have often wondered how much suffering that involved." Paul nodded somberly. "Human history," he said, "is filled with misery and suffering. Only in God do we find peace."

I thought that was my cue. "Poor Thessaloniki," I said. "She had three sons. One died young; the other two ruled together. But one of them killed his own mother in the end."

I remember Paul looking very serious. "So much violence," he said, "in all the nations. Only our Lord Jesus Christ proclaimed peace." He turned to my father. "I also thought that violence would bring an end to the way of Jesus," he said, and I heard sorrow in his voice. "I was a zealot, thinking I was doing the will of God when I persecuted Christians. Then the Lord Jesus appeared to me and asked me not to persecute him any longer but to serve him. I have never lifted a finger in anger against anyone since that moment."

I was intrigued by his story. Later I went to Timotheos, who was much younger than the other two, and said, "I too want to see Jesus." Timotheos smiled and said that he had the same longing. "The closest I have come to seeing the Lord Jesus," he told me, "is in the person of Paul himself. One day you will feel the same." Today I understand Timotheos's meaning.

In those early days our entire family was enthralled by Paul and his words. We were soon baptized in the faith. So many followed our example, our house was always full. There were native Macedonians among us, Greeks from the south who had settled in our beautiful city, many Romans—Thessaloniki being the capital of the province—and a good number of Jews. All groups were represented in the *ekklesia* that was formed after Paul's preaching. We met in each other's homes, but ours was the largest and it became a kind of a hub for the activities of the new believers. It was a time of discovering the truth and responding to it with joy.

When the troubles started with the merchants and the priests of the cults, and they dragged Paul and his partners before the *politarch*, we all helped to shelter them. My father came to the aid of Jason, their loyal Jewish host, when his house was attacked by the mob looking for Paul. My father and Jason were taken to the authorities and father assisted Jason when he was ordered to pay bail. My mother and our friends hid our three guests while others arranged to lead the apostles out of the city in the dark of the night.

We had spent several months with Paul, Silvanus, and Timotheos. When they left we were bereft. We all cried as we said goodbye. Even Paul's eyes were filled with tears. I remember the torches lighting the dear faces of our friends, the whispered voices, the quick hugs and kisses, and then the darkness as they slipped into the night. My father took them to the western gate of the city, and we heard that they had escaped safely to travel the next day to Berea.

I longed to see Paul again and to hear his voice, but my father had that privilege. Since he was involved in the agora, the marketplace, he knew what was going on. When he learned that agitators were planning to go to Berea to cause trouble for Paul, my father left ahead of them and went to warn our friends. When he returned from Berea we learned that Paul had been sent to Athens ahead of the others.

Paul's first letter arrived to us from Corinth and we were jubilant. Paul was convinced that the Lord's return was imminent during those early years. But for us, the sweetest reassurance was in how much Paul loved us. By that time, several of our men, my father among them, had been flogged for believing and testifying in the name of Jesus Christ. Paul's letter gave us the strength to persevere.

Timotheos finally returned to bring us Paul's news from Corinth and to take our news back to him. He stayed in our home. It was again a time of celebration because we felt connected with many new Christians in all of Greece. And throughout these long years, when Paul traveled tirelessly from Corinth to Ephesos and other places in Asia, he sent us news, longing to be with us again. He did come one more time to bring us strength and to fortify us in the Lord. Always, always, we were assured of his great love for us in Thessaloniki.

News of his last voyage to Rome and his strange desire to testify before the emperor troubled many of us who know something of the emperor's madness. Aristarchos kept us informed of the storms and shipwrecks, of the floggings and imprisonments that Paul suffered for his faith. When my whole family was thrown into prison, we sang and praised God as Paul had always done. The thought that he would be pleased with us was a comfort. *(She pauses and collects herself. She is ready to reveal something vital.)*

But last night I could find no comfort. I closed myself in my room and wept aloud for a long while. I felt that with Paul's death something terrible had befallen all of us. During those hours of intense grief, I could not believe in God's love. I could not imagine that the Christian churches would find the strength to survive what is coming. Paul had always warned us of a great persecution, and I knew last night that the hour had come for us to be tested.

In my abject grief, when all seemed dark within and without, I became aware of a presence in the room. It was as real as you are at this moment, sitting here around me, listening to me. *(She reaches out and touches the person closest to her.)* I had lit no lamps and I was sitting in darkness. Suddenly the room was no longer dark; light was radiating from the presence. I stopped crying and fell on my knees. I waited. I heard a voice. "Daughter," the voice said, "you have longed to see my face. You have seen me in Paul, you have seen me in your other brothers and sisters. Be not afraid. I will not abandon you."

I prostrated myself before this vision, a great peace flooding and surrounding me. I recognized that the face that came to me in the vision may have been Paul's, but much younger and more radiant. The voice was not Paul's, but it was a voice that I recognized. This is a mystery. I cannot explain it in any other way. All I know is that it took away doubt and gave me the assurance of love. I have not shed a tear since that moment. I woke all in the house to tell them about my vision. I have decided to visit every *ekklesia* in our vicinity to reassure them of Christ's love and of his promise to remain with us always.

The days of tribulation have arrived. Aristarchos testified that Paul met his death without a hint of fear. He had become so popular in Rome that the soldiers found it impossible to keep him in any constraints. They knew that, because he had given them his word, he would never escape.

Paul brought the good news of Jesus Christ to countless people in Rome. And he did it from his house prison. Aristarchos told us that when Nero sent for Paul, the soldiers who accompanied him were weeping aloud. Paul prayed with them and blessed them. Even at the end, he was thinking of his flock. He told Aristarchos to urge his brothers and sisters to go into hiding because Nero was planning a terrible death for them. The soldiers told the Christians who stood outside the place of death that Paul blessed even his executioner and offered him his forgiveness. Then he walked to his death in peace, praying unceasingly.

When Aristarchos reached Ostia, he heard that Rome was burning. We don't know how many of our sisters and brothers perished in the fire. But I came here to tell you that Paul lives as Christ lives. He sent us a note. Listen: "I am persuaded that neither death, nor life, nor angels, nor rulers, not things present, nor things to come, nor power, nor height, nor depth, nor anything else in all creation will be able to separate us from the love of God in Christ Jesus our Lord."

Questions to Ponder

1. The young woman from Thessaloniki mentions "the greed of everyone associated with pagan idols." What role does greed play in our society today? What examples of greed associated with Christianity can you cite?

2. How do you think you would live out your faith if you were subject to persecution as the early Christians were?

3. The young woman says, "During those hours of intense grief, I could not believe in God's love." Have you experienced a grief so deep that you doubted God's love, or even God's existence? How did you resolve your doubt?

4. Have you found specific ways to reassure others of God's love for them? If so, what are they? Why do you think such reassurance is important?

5. Why does the narrator insist on telling the new Christians that the face she saw of Christ may have been that of Paul? Why did she recognize the voice even though it did not belong to Paul?

Bibliography

Meyers, Carol, Toni Craven and Ross S. Kraemer, eds. *Women in Scripture*. Boston: Houghton Mifflin Co., 2000.

Morison, Frank. *Who Moved the Stone?* Grand Rapids: Zondervan Publishing House, 1958. (First edition copyright by Albert Henry Ross, 1930.)

Sayers, Dorothy L. *The Man Born to Be King: A Play-Cycle on the Life of Our Lord and Saviour Jesus Christ*. Grand Rapids: William B. Eerdmans, 1974. (First edition copyright by Dorothy L. Sayers, 1943.)

Temple, William. *Readings in Saint John's Gospel*. Harrisburg, Penn.: Morehouse Publishing, 1985.

The New Oxford Annotated Bible with the Apocrypha. New Revised Standard Version. New York: Oxford University Press, 1991.

Η ΚΑΙΝΗ ΔΙΑΘΗΚΗ. Text with Critical Apparatus. London: The British and Foreign Bible Society, 1904.

Katerina Whitley enjoys presenting these monologues to groups, and is a popular retreat leader and presenter for church programs and other meetings. You may contact her through Morehouse Publishing or e-mail her at katewhitley@earthlink.net.

Comments from those who have seen her presentations already:

"The crowd was spellbound. The insights she brought to biblical women touch each of us with new understanding and emotions. Her scholarship is beyond question."

—Bates Toone, Coordinator for Christian Formation, Diocese of Kentucky

"For the first time I realized that these were living breathing women! I will read the Bible with new eyes from now on."

—Katie Westervelt, student at East Carolina University